Legends of
GOLF

AND OTHER OBSERVATIONS ON THE GAME

Louis Stanley (left) with Ben Hogan in Christ Church, Oxford, in 1949. Sadly on 25 July 1997 Ben Hogan died in Fort Worth, Texas, aged 84. The game has lost its perfectionist whose dedication set standards that have never been surpassed. He was the complete player. A rare man and a friend.

Legends of GOLF

AND OTHER OBSERVATIONS ON THE GAME

LOUIS T. STANLEY

FOREWORD BY FRANK STRANAHAN

PUBLISHED BY

SALAMANDER BOOKS LIMITED

LONDON

A SALAMANDER BOOK

This edition published in 1997 by SMITHMARK Publishers, a division of U.S. Media Holdings, Inc., 115 West 18th Street, New York, NY 10011.

3 5 7 9 8 6 4 2

SMITHMARK books are available for bulk purchase for sales promotion and premium use. For details write or call the manager of special sales, SMITHMARK Publishers, 115 West 18th Street, New York, NY 10011.

All correspondence concerning the content of this book should be addressed to Salamander Books Ltd., 8 Blenheim Court, Brewery Road, London N7 9NT, United Kingdom.

ISBN 0-7651-1656-1

CREDITS

Editor: Richard Collins; Designer: Mark Holt
All photographs supplied by the author
Filmset: SX Composing Ltd, England; Mono reproduction: Pixel Tech Ltd, Singapore
Printed in France

THE AUTHOR

Over a period of years Louis Stanley's writing on golf has been noted for its authority, warmth and penetration. He has the enviable knack of capturing a personality in a pen portrait and of recalling the atmosphere of the big occasion, be it St Andrews, Hoylake, Muirfield, Westward Ho!, Sandwich, Aberdovey, Lelant, or championship courses in America.

Garry Player once wrote: "Louis Stanley, a scratch golfer, has studied, analyzed and played with many of the greatest players...in fact, no player of international repute has escaped the lens of his camera." Henry Cotton added, "Louis Stanley writes more words about the golf game than any other writer I know, and whilst he turned to golfing matters as a hobby, he applies what lies beyond that deep forehead of his in studying golf intensely...a scratch golfer himself...how he finds time to play golf so well is yet another mystery..." Cyril Tolley, one of Britain's greatest Amateur champions, commented, "One has to go back many years to recall when the tall stalwart figure of Louis Stanley first appeared on the great championship links, moving unhurriedly through the galleries...not only is he a fine scratch golfer, but without fear of contradiction Louis Stanley is a peer among action photographers."

Then followed a break in continuity. Louis Stanley absented himself from the golf scene and exchanged the links for motor racing circuits. As Chairman and joint-Managing Director with his wife, Jean, they directed the family owned BRM racing car to victory in the Formula One World Championship as well as winning most of that sport's major honors. Among his drivers were Fangio, Peter Collins, Mike Hawthorn, Graham Hill, Jackie Stewart and Niki Lauda. His other responsibilities included Director-General of the International Grand Prix Medical Service – he was instrumental in improving medical facilities on European and American circuits and his Mobile Hospital saved many lives; Honorary Secretary and Treasurer of the Grand Prix Drivers Association; Chairman of the Siffert Council; and Trustee of the Jim Clark Foundation.

ACKNOWLEDGEMENTS

I greatly appreciate the contributions by Frank Stranahan and Robert Halsall which brought back vivid memories of years ago. I am also indebted to the editors of *Golf Monthly* for their courteous permission to reprint certain extracts.

Contents

Frank Stranahan, the only man to win every major Amateur Championship in the world, being congratulated by King George VI in 1948.

Foreword

Louis Stanley asked me to write the Foreword for his *Legends of Golf*. This will be his eighty-second book. I feel honoured.

It is fascinating to learn of his many varied interests from being a Cambridge economist and industrialist with outstanding success including the Formula 1 World Championship title with the famous racing car BRM. In the process every European and American honour was collected. Add to this Louis' pioneering work that made the world's circuits safer for the Grand Prix drivers. He has touched the fringe of many further achievements. When one finds and can pursue an area where he or she can give a *total commitment*, life can be very satisfying. Louis has been able to accomplish this feat in many different fields.

To read his book and see how thoroughly Louis Stanley captures every aspect of golf in Great Britain, the United States and around the world is absolutely astounding. He takes his readers into the history of golf, from its beginning up to a startling knowledge of Tiger Woods and the present. *Legends of Golf* covers the outstanding amateurs and professionals around the world, plus a special insight into St Andrews (home of the Royal and Ancient), the Masters in Augusta, Georgia, the Ryder Cup matches, and a very interesting analysis of various Champions and their swings. It is difficult to fathom the research effort that went into his marvellous treatise. Our favourite game certainly owes Louis Stanley an enormous debt of gratitude for the massive workload he assumes and administrates in connection with its many facets.

Speaking for myself, progressive exercise with weights, running and fasting are the most wonderful discoveries that I have ever made. Since I have not touched a golf club in over ten years, my present interests are finance, training with weights, and longevity.

A careful study of your manuscript brought back a flood of nostalgic memories, Louis, and you may be sure that I shall place these in my 'Archives of Memorabilia'.

I sincerely hope that our paths will cross before too long!

Golfingly yours

Frank R. Stranahan
JULY 1997

Introduction

It gives me great pleasure to write an introduction to this
wonderful new book *Legends of Golf*.
I remember vividly seeing Louis for the first time at his own
great club, Royal Liverpool. It was April 1930. I had been
invited by Harry Bentley and his father, known as Pa. I was to
caddy for Harry, who at that stage, was one of the best amateur
golfers in England. As we moved to the practise ground, we
passed the first tee. There stood a tall, elegant young man,
possibly a couple of years older than myself, swinging a club
with a great deal of panache. I thought to myself, if he could
repeat the movement when the ball was there, it would be
something and my God, he did. Rarely have I seen such power
generated in a golf swing. I thought to myself, I shall walk up
the fairway with him to see him play his second. This time, the
same swing but with something like a seven or eight iron which
was despatched to within six feet from the pin, and don't
forget this was with a hickory shaft. I watched him play
another fantastic tee shot from the second before heading back
to the practise ground. I said, "You've got your work cut out
today Harry – who is that player moving down the second
fairway?" He said, "That's Louis Stanley, a member of
Hoylake." What a glorious course Hoylake was at that time and
I was privileged to see Bobby Jones win The Open there later
in that same year.
I remember at one stage, my old pal Henry Cotton being rather
jealous of Louis and the quality of his books. Although Henry
himself wrote some very fine golfing books, in my opinion, they
didn't quite compare to Louis' professional work. The source of
annoyance to Henry was that the author's notes to Louis' books
always carried the label "scratch golfer" and I remember once
being in Henry's company when he complained, "But nobody's
ever seen him hit a ball." I had to say, "I'm sorry Henry – I
have seen him play and I can tell you, he's a very fine player
indeed."After my commendation, Henry changed his opinion
and gave him full recognition for the quality of his work. Like
Henry Cotton and myself, Louis was an advocate of the
importance of hands in the golf swing and I remember in our
golf school in Monte Carlo, Henry had posted on the wall the
words "Your golf is as good as your hands. Your style is as good
as your hands."

Why is this game so difficult? Undoubtedly, the golf swing is not a natural movement. However, you will see readers, in the many photographs that Louis Stanley has taken, that the great golfers of our time have overcome the limitations of nature. Louis and I are agreed that the hands are a dominant influence in overcoming nature's resistance and the pictures in this book will support that theory.

Every Open Championship or Tournament, Louis Stanley would be there, complete with his Leica camera hanging from his neck, and not forgetting his shooting stick which was always omnipresent on such occasions. In my own honest opinion, nobody has taken better action photographs and then been able to explain in beautiful prose the movements he had photographed. He merely loved to wander around the course taking snaps of all the players, not just the good ones, mind you, even I appeared in one or two of his earlier books! I have talked to many pros over the years who have told me that they have learned an enormous amount just by studying the detailed action photographs he has taken. Indeed, I have never forgotten reading his book *This is Golf* and I am convinced it helped me to finish fifteenth in the Open Championship at my own course, Royal Birkdale, in 1954. Prize money £30!

Louis has published some great books but this one, encompassing as it does all the legends of our time, is likely to surpass them all. I was in Monte Carlo this winter when a golf pro approached me about acquiring some of Louis' earlier works as they are fetching premium prices and are virtually unobtainable. This book is a wonderful compilation of the great golfers who have previously figured in Louis' books and I feel privileged to be associated with such a work of art. I will certainly be taking a few copies with me to Monte Carlo next winter!

Bobby Halsall

July 1997

Robert Halsall was for many years professional at the Royal Birkdale Golf Club and the Monte Carlo Golf Club; for many people the golf pro par excellence.

Lakeside: Upsets in Championship Golf

Although it does not rival the lush foliage and profusion of floral extravagance of Augusta, I regard the Lakeside course of the Olympic Country Club as one of the most beautiful golf courses in the United States. It all began in 1922 when the Olympic Club bought a somewhat featureless golf course on the western side of San Francisco alongside the Pacific Ocean. With long-term foresight the course was transformed by framing every hole with eucalyptus, pine and cypress trees. The plan worked. The trees, now matured into majestic forest size, dictate shot-making. Any slip and the ball is swallowed up. The prevailing wind blows off the Pacific, but the tree-cover makes it swirl in unpredictable fashion. Apart from the four short holes, the sinuous nature of the layout leaves hardly a straight line. If second shots are to be trouble-free, accurate tee-shot placing is essential. The hooker or player who likes to draw long drives from right to left can be in real trouble. In summer, mists rolling in from the Bay at night keep moisture on the greens. Compared with other championship tests, the course is on the short side, but it plays very long and makes an exacting examination. This has been emphasized in a big way when it has hosted the United States Open Championship with a dramatic climax that confounded all predictions.

In 1966 the title looked as good as won on the 9th green when Arnold Palmer was seven strokes up on Billy Casper and nine up on Jack Nicklaus. It was a psychological boost at a critical time in Palmer's career for it was two years since he had won a major championship. The idol of Arnie's Army suddenly had feet of clay and he knew it. He was the sad oyster that could not produce the pearl. The threat at Lakeside came from Billy Casper, a tough opponent who seemed permanently miffed about not receiving true public rating or recognition. He was categorized as quarrelsome and introverted but all had changed. Casper had found religion, joined the Church of Jesus Christ of the Latter-day Saints and was giving some four Mormon services a week wherever he happened to be. He was also preoccupied with the problems of allergies and had acquired a taste for pan-fried whale, buffalo steak and ground elk. A practical result was the loss of some 50lb, while professionals said that in tournaments it was like playing a mystic. It certainly aided his powers of recovery in the Open.

At the 13th Palmer was six up with six to play. Nicklaus had dropped out of contention. On the 191 yard par 3 fourteenth Palmer missed the green The lead was cut to five. At the 15th, a 150 yard short-iron, Palmer went for the flag, but caught the right bunker. Casper carded a birdie. On the 16th tee Palmer was three up with three to go. Four strokes had been lopped off his lead. A typical Palmer flourish was needed. He settled for a right-to-left drive, hooked violently and finished in the deep rough. He failed to recover with a 3 iron, wedged to the fairway, put the next in a bunker, one putt and six on the card. Casper had a birdie. The lead now down to one. At the 17th Palmer again hooked sharply into the rough, recovery hesitant, putt missed. Casper one-putted for par. The seven-stroke lead had evaporated in eight holes. Palmer used an iron from the 18th tee, still missed the fairway, but played a wedge out of thick rough to the edge of the green. Both made par.

In the play off, Palmer out in 33 held a two-stroke lead, but Casper clawed them back by the 11th. Palmer cracked. His card read par, par, one over, one over, two over, and the Open was won by Casper with 69 to 73.

If the unbelievable defeat of Arnold Palmer was a shock, it was nothing to the upset that occurred in the closing stages of the 1955 Open. It centred round Ben Hogan who had attained a peak of perfection in his mastery of shot making. In 1948 he won eleven tournaments, including the United States Open with an all-time low of 276, and a second United

Right: Billy Casper will never forget his Olympic Club victory in 1966. Seven strokes behind Palmer with nine holes to play, he tied and won the play-off by four shots.

Right: Contenders at the Olympic Club included Julius Boros (left), the oldest winner of the US Open in 1963, and Gene Littler (right), former US Open in 1961 and Amateur champion in 1953.

States PGA title. Everything pointed to domination of the golfing scene when a near fatal crash with a truck in the fog threatened to terminate his playing career in 1949. Recovery was near miraculous. Later that year he came to England as non-playing captain of the American Ryder Cup team. The after-effects of convalescence were traumatic and painful. When the team arrived at Southampton on the *Queen Elizabeth*, a convoy of Rolls-Royce cars waited to take us to the Savoy Hotel in London. I was in the leading car with Hogan, but after a few miles it became obvious that he was far from happy. Accustomed to the flow of traffic on a different side of the road, he was tensed by the thought of a possible collision with each approaching car. The best thing was to drop behind at the tail of the convoy. The journey by road continued next day, broken by breaks for coffee with the dons of Christ Church, Oxford, an official lunch at Stratford-upon-Avon, finally arriving somewhat weary at the Grand Hotel in Scarborough. Hogan stood the journey well, but was in constant pain with a tight rubber suit under his clothes. Even walking caused distress, yet never once did the galleries know of the discomfort.

Determination worked wonders. Instead of watching from a wheel-chair like a semi-invalid, Hogan came back to the tournament scene, but not in token appearances. He won three national championships in 1953, finished first in five events he entered, including his second Masters at Augusta, added a fourth United States Open title, and added the Open Championship at Carnoustie on his first attempt, and not forgetting his third PGA title. Never has a patient made such a

recovery. Then at the Olympic Club he thought his last ambition had been real-ized, to be the first to win the US title five times, to stand alone in the record books above Bobby Jones and Willie Anderson, both of whom had won four. When his last putt dropped for an aggregate of 287, the title looked won. Gene Sarazen rushed forward with a hand microphone. In an interview beamed across the States, Hogan was congratulated on achieving the near impossible. He responded by holding up an outspread right hand, the splayed five fingers symbolizing the feat. A national television audience was left to believe the title had been clinched and the network returned to regular programming. Hogan even gave the ball to Joe Dey, executive director of the US PGA, to be put in the official museum in New York.

Right: Ben Hogan holds up an outstretched right hand with fingers hopefully splayed, symbolizing the feat of winning five Open titles.

Then the news seeped through that a 1000–1 outsider had a remote chance to tie. A couple of hours behind Ben Hogan, Jack Fleck was playing a lonely round without spectators. The man was unknown. Son of a Iowa truck farmer, his introduction to the game came in 1936 when he watched Ralph Guldahl win the Western Open on the Davenport Country Club course. Later he got a job there caddying and taught himself to play on Mondays when cad-dies were allowed to use the course. After graduating from high school, Fleck went to work full-time as an assistant in the pro shop. By 1954 he had become manager and professional at Davenport's two municipal courses, located eight miles apart, and com-muted between them. In 1955 he left his wife Lynn to look after the shops and joined the winter–spring Tour for the first time.

On track record Fleck stood no chance at Lakeside, but the figures that came through suggested it was just possible. A birdie at the 15th, fol-lowed by par, par, left a birdie needed to tie. On the last tee the lanky professional walloped his drive into the rough. That was that. It had been a wonderful effort, but it meant Hogan had won. We underestimated the outsider. Very calmly he played a magnificent recovery that reached the green.

I asked Fleck afterwards what were his thoughts at that crucial moment. His recollection was vague except for the thought he had to swing the club without forcing. The putt, about 30 feet, must have looked a mile. Without any signs of nerves, Fleck studied the line. The green tilted sharply from back to front and its surface was slippery, so much so that throughout the Championship players had been babying their putts, hoping to catch a corner of the cup. He stroked the ball

Left: Jack Fleck's famous putt at the 1955 Open. The "unknown" studied the line and struck the ball as calmly as if a dollar were at stake. The ball dropped in the tin. Fleck raised both arms, swayed as if to collapse. Ed Furgol, who had just seen his title disappear, took Fleck under his wing and led him to the locker-room. He said afterwards that he knew what it was like to be in such a mental whirl.

solidly, watched it curl slightly downhill, and drop into the centre of the hole, birdie 3 for 67 and a tie with Hogan, a fantastic finish because it was so unexpected.

Fleck raised both arms in excitement, swayed, and looked as if he would collapse. Police escorted him to the official tent. He had played himself out. The first to appreciate the situation was Ed Furgol, the defending champion, who had just seen his title disappear. He took Fleck under his care, led him off to the locker room, saw that he recovered, went with him to the Press Room and helped with the answers. Furgol said afterwards that he had been in a similar position himself the year before and knew something of Fleck's mental whirl. In the Championship Furgol had tied for 45th place.

The play off was expected to be one-sided. I thought Hogan would apply pressure and win by a comfortable margin. The prediction was way out. At the final hole Fleck led by one stroke. Hogan pulled his teeshot into the rough through a foot slipping on the tee. The ball was barely visible in the lush grass.

Right: Ike Grainger, then President of the United States Golf Association, is remembered as an influential legislator of the game.

The recovery shot shifted it a foot. Hogan swung again. The ball moved three feet. The green was only 130 yards away, but a sideways shot was the only choice. Eventually the green was reached some 30 feet above the hole. Hogan recorded a 6, but Fleck, on in 2, two-putted for a solid par and won by 3 strokes. Jack Fleck, the unknown, was Open Champion. Of the six sub-par rounds played in the Championship, he had recorded two of them, and through his red-hot Hogan putter, had managed one more.

Fleck was in a daze. Later we met in the St Francis Hotel. Because the United Nations was in session for its tenth anniversary and the sixth floor had become the equivalent of the White House, Fleck said that the day before he was nobody, an unknown professional, the John Doe of golf. Now he was the Open Champion and had been congratulated by the President. It was an experience out of fiction. But what of Ben Hogan? His bid to stand alone in the record book had aborted. The chances of succeeding in the future were slight. That night I dined in Trader Vic's on Fisherman's Wharf with Ben and Valerie Hogan and Bing Crosby and his wife. Ben was unstinting in praise of Fleck. It was sincere recognition of his fighting qualities. He later put it into practice by helping Fleck to readjust to the new role. This gesture from a man who was usually unemotional gave a glimpse of a hidden side of his nature. Ben Hogan has that intangible quality which we call genius. His enthusiasm for the game has not waned. His methods have not dated. He stands alone. Sadly Jack Fleck has faded into obscurity, but Ben Hogan is the senior statesman of the game, a legend of achievement.

Left: Fleck, who dreamt he had won the Open, found it a reality. His presentation speech was short but emotional. Hogan's reaction (he stands second from left, front row, applauding the winner) was warm and generous.

2
Problem Behaviour

Global golf is flourishing at every level, which can only be good. At the same time disturbing traits have surfaced that from time to time run counter to the traditions of the game. I refer to the growing tendency of partisan spectators applauding mistakes made by a player they hope will be beaten. Instances come to mind like the Dunhill Cup at St Andrews when Nick Faldo declined to play an important approach shot to the 18th green when it was shrouded in fog. His decision was accepted by referee and opponent Des Smyth, but spectators rowdily voiced disapproval. When Faldo missed the vital putt next morning, onlookers were not slow to register delight. Officials deplored the behaviour with vague warnings that steps would be taken to prevent a recurrence of such loutish outbursts in the future, while yet another organizer declared that in all his years he had never heard anything like it before, knowingly speculating how Tom Morris would have reacted. I can only imagine this gentleman must have led a sheltered life and was somewhat weak on golfing history.

Obviously partisan barracking is deplorable and any measures to check it are welcome, but, human nature being what it is, I fear that these are paper threats. In closely contested championship and international events with a title or result in the balance, every shot is vital, even decisive. Such a situation inevitably divides galleries into supporters. The relief when a crucial putt fails to drop induces audible relief, sometimes sufficiently vociferous to distract the unfortunate fellow who has missed the shot. It is not personal, but at that moment a section is willing him to lose. Some spectators, never particularly articulate, resort to the behaviour of the terraces. Golfing etiquette means nothing. Such an attitude is alien to the

Right: Bobby Locke, slim young man, on his first visit to England.

game, but it is naïve to suggest the phenomenon is new. It has always been there, only today it has increased.

Think of that British victory in the Ryder Cup match at Lindrick in 1957 when the course echoed to partisan cheers as miracles began to happen on that last afternoon. Recall how roughly Paul Azinger was treated in the 1987 Open at Muirfield when he lost the title on the last green. Ironically the winner was Nick Faldo. The young American took the abrasive incidents in his stride. His only comment was a dignified rebuke that Faldo was the "slowest man on earth".

Returning to the Dunhill outburst, it must be remembered that spectators and the media have long memories. Today Faldo has matured into an outstanding competitive professional, but before reaching this level of excellence he had been known to blot his copybook. There was the occasion when Sandy Lyle used sticking-tape to stop the glare of the Nairobi sun on his putter head. Faldo reported him and Lyle was disqualified. Then there was the occasion when Faldo's ball was thrown back on the green during a World Match Play tie with the Australian, Graham Marsh. Faldo accepted the referee's ruling, but did not concede his opponent a 3 foot putt which Marsh missed to lose the hole. On both occasions the actions were within the rules but at the expense of the spirit of the law.

A regrettable incident occurred at the Gulfstream World International at Loch Mond a few days before the 1997 Open Championship at Troon. Nick Faldo had a tantrum over apparent imperfections in his golf clubs. Spectators heard the professional hurl abuse at employees of Mizuno, the equipment company that supplies his clubs. It really is no excuse to talk of patience levels being thin. Further, it is no excuse for a player of Faldo's stature to fly into a rage with a flow of obscenities in front of spectators. Such conduct as this simply brings the game into disrepute.

As regards the horrified reaction of the Dunhill official and the invoking of Tom Morris's indignation, let me recall an incident which happened in 1855 when Willie Park and Tom Morris were playing the fifth of a series of six £100 challenge matches at Musselburgh, which was refereed by the Edinburgh publisher, Robert Chambers. Feelings began to run high and partisan spectators continually interfered with Morris's ball. Eventually, things got so bad that Morris and Chambers sought sanctuary in Mrs Forman's pub and refused to come out,

Left: Nick Faldo, single-minded "rookie", determined to make the grade.

*Right: Severiano
Ballesteros, uninhibited
at the outset of his
career.*

whereupon Park sent a message to say that he would play the remaining holes by
himself and claim the match. The refugees stayed in the pub and were held to
have forfeited the stakes. At least Faldo did not have to retreat to Rusacks.

Another occasion, also in Scotland, was in the 1925 Open at Prestwick.
Macdonald Smith, the expatriate from Carnoustie, long resident in America, and
one of the finest swingers of a golf club at that time, was poised to win the Championship. Rounds of 76, 69 and 76 meant that 78 would bring victory. Enormous
crowds of supporters, many non-paying, turned out to see the Scot win. Such was
their eagerness to watch every shot that the jostling led to a round of 82 and the
title went to Jim Barnes.

Vigorous attempts have been made by the Royal and Ancient Club to curb
partisanship, but it is difficult, if not impossible. There are bound to be spasmodic

outbursts of misguided patriotism whenever the Ryder Cup match is played at The Belfry or in Spain with Ballesteros trying to win the Cup for the king in his native Spain. Conceivably similar outbursts will occur when the Open is staged.

There is another side to the problem. Maybe professionals are becoming over-sensitive. The Centre Court at Wimbledon has its quota of temperamental outbursts from the competitors themselves; penalty kickers at Rugby Union matches at Twickenham, Murrayfield, Cardiff Arms Park and Lansdowne Road have to endure a crescendo of shrill whistling at critical moments; several other sports are marred by interruptions. Professional golfers must accept the fact that they are public entertainers receiving monetary rewards out of all proportion to their talents, though not in the same league as Formula One racing drivers whose retainers have reached levels that are obscene. Any sport that justifies such earnings becomes primarily a commercial enterprise dictated by Big Business. It ceases to be a sport as the term is understood.

Left: Tommy Bolt, the fiery American professional, known for tantrums. Ill-temper cost him dear. On one occasion his caddie explained why he had advised a restrained two iron instead of Bolt's preference for a nine iron by saying that there were only two irons left in the bag.

This applies to the game of golf. In 1989 the potential earnings on the European circuit totalled £11.66 million, a figure that has increased every year. Sponsors are anxious to pour cash into the coffers. The effect on the game is reflected in the Open Championship. Everything about this historic event has changed. The so-called tented village is awash with traders, entrepreneurs, public relations types, itinerant traders, anyone out to make a buck. Amid all this bazaar-like activity hospitality facilities attract non-golfing clients enjoying sponsor patronage. The ordinary spectator is left to wonder whether he or she is being short-changed. Entrance fees have become extortionate with countless petty restrictions curtailing freedom of movement and viewing. The Royal and Ancient does a magnificent job in organizing, but sadly its preoccupation is the bottom line. The priorities of its official role has become too commercial. I only wish we had a golfing ombudsman.

One official who became exasperated was Frank Hannigan, former Chief Executive of the United States Golf Association. Possibly irritated by the behaviour of a professional as he plied his trade or the attitude of his agent, Hannigan caustically commented, "If the world of professional golf gathered for one of its multi-million junkets in California and an earthquake swept them all into the sea, the rest of the world would express sympathy, observe one minute silence, and then carry on as before." I am afraid he was right. The game would continue to flourish in less exotic fashion.

Putting aside such morbid thoughts by the USGA, it is interesting to recall how the professional scene in this country has changed. In 1950, fifty-seven players in Britain shared £21,048 of the £27,000 prize-money earmarked for home tournaments. Seven professionals netted from £1,000 to £2,000 between them. Economies were in the air. The Ryder Cup team travelled cabin class in the *Queen Mary* and saved the PGA approximately £1,250. The following year the stake money was £25,000, but in 1952 it fell to £24,340 from fourteen major tournaments. Should some reader imagine that the professionals who fought for spoils

that today would be pin-money were repaid for their skill, the answer is that men like Bobby Locke, Fred Daly, Peter Thomson and Henry Cotton were, shot for shot, every bit as good as the likes of Faldo, Woosnam, Montgomerie, Lehram or Els, often far better shot-makers than these pampered millionaires. Such criticism does not decry the immense pleasure enjoyed by millions of television viewers who watch their skills without thought of their inflated financial rewards.

To get away from carping, it is soothing to watch a traditional amateur event. One such is the President's Putter at Rye. Everything about this fixture is unpredictable. To hold a tournament in January is tempting fate. Invariably the weather is bitterly cold with biting winds and arctic temperatures, yet it is rare for the elements to halt proceedings. There have been exceptions when snow wins. I recall stocks of red balls becoming exhausted. Even the emergency supply of balls painted red with the professional's wife nail-varnish disappeared. The overall figure was 200 abandoned balls. Some players resorted to an 8-iron off the tee in the hope of locating the shot. Although the fairways were difficult, the greens remained playable. Wisely the committee decided the competition would be completed during a weekend in March and sixteen shivering golfers returned to their homes, but somehow it was not the same. All very civilized and amateurish, but that is what golf is all about. It is a game to be enjoyed in convivial company.

Left: Peter Thomson came to prominence in the 1950s and 1960s, his finest achievements being at the Open. Runner-up to Bobby Locke in 1952 at the age of twenty-two, he took the prize at Royal Birkdale in 1954.

3
Persona Grata

Right: Lord Brabazon of Tara (in front of the microphones) was outstanding in many fields of activity.

A remarkable man in many, many ways, *Lord Brabazon of Tara* achieved so much in so many different fields that the term *unique* might be correctly applied. It is hard to describe his influence to anyone who did not feel the impact of his personality. He was the personification of thoroughness. He could be as crude and direct as a television interviewer, and had a fierce line in glares, plus a penetrating voice.

He held the Aviator's Certificate No. 1 of the Fédération Aeronautique Internationale dated 8 March 1910. Some thirty years later he marked that occasion by securing a personal car number FLY 1. He won the £1,000 prize offered by the *Daily Mail* for a circular flight of one mile by flying a hotch-potch of a flying machine at an average height of 40 feet. He won the Circuit d'Ardennes in 1907 in a Minerva, and was not only one of the earliest riders on the Cresta toboggan run, but the oldest when he was in his seventies. In World War I he pioneered aerial photography.

In the House of Commons, Brab left many stories, such as his reference to the Opposition as "a lot of inverted Micawbers waiting for something to turn down". In "another place" he dismissed the Archbishop of Canterbury's comments on finance as "talking through his mitre". During the war Brabazon was Minister of Transport, then in charge of Aircraft Production. He was also President of the Royal Institution. His value on a golf committee was that of a probe, highlighting the inefficiency of many of his colleagues, but he was always ready for a light aside. I recall when he sat next to me at an Executive Meeting of the English Golf Union. He offered me a cigar, then a cigarette, followed by tobacco and finally snuff before accepting the fact that I was a non-smoker.

Brabazon caused consternation among the caddies at St Andrews when he took the first caddie-car around the Old Course. Their concern was understandable. It was a threat to their livelihood. Not long afterwards the post of Links caddie-master was discontinued, happily restored by the Links Trust. It was a remarkable background crowned by his appointment as Captain of the Royal and Ancient Golf Club. That satisfaction was reflected in his autobiography when he summarized, "When I look back on my life and try to decide out of what I have got more actual pleasure, I have no doubt at all that I have got more out of golf than anything else."

I always associate *Raymond Oppenheimer* with the University match at Hoylake in 1927. The weather was atrocious. A gale swept across the fairways, and I was one of the few who watched his terrific struggle against Grimwade which went to the forty-first hole. Following that, Oppenheimer's influence on the game was considerable. He captained the Old Harrovians when they won the Halford Hewitt Cup; British selector in 1947 and 1949, Walker Cup captain in 1951. He played a leading part in the development of golf among youths. Active business partner in the Oppenheimer empire, I recall lunching with him at their City headquarters; he went to a cabinet and drew out one of the display drawers. It held several hundred sparking diamonds!

Left: Raymond Oppenheimer – British Walker Cup Captain in 1951; English international; leading breeder of bull terriers.

Peter Guthrie Tait, professor of philosophy and mathematician at Edinburgh University, had a life-long affection for St Andrews. From 1868 he stayed there every summer for some thirty years and was a member of the Royal and Ancient Club for thirty six-years. His enthusiasm for golf was remarkable. Five rounds a day over the Old Course meant a start about 6 a.m., a routine which would tax the stamina of the fittest and was certainly too much for the caddies who worked on a shift basis. John Low aptly described the Professor as "the oldest boy and the youngest old man we ever knew". Low, who was one of the founders of the Oxford and Cambridge Golfing Society and Chairman of the Rules of Golf Committee for twenty years, also recorded one of the lighter moment's of Tait's golfing activities: " . . . In 1871 the meeting of the British Association was held in Edinburgh, the Professor being President of Section A. After the proceedings were finished some of the most distinguished members of the assembly accompanied him to St Andrews. Among them were Huxley, Helmholtz, Andrews and Sylvester . . . It is the dinner hour and the Professor proposes to the company that a round may be played with phosphorescent balls. When the proper arrangements were made, the party assembled at the first teeing-ground. To this match come the Professor and his lady; Huxley, keen on the humour of the thing; Professor Crum Brown and another friend. The idea is a success; the balls glisten in the grass and advertise their situation; the players make strokes which surprise their opponents and apprise themselves of hitherto unknown powers. All goes well till the burn is passed. Professor Crum Brown's hand is found to be aflame; with difficulty his burning glove is unbuttoned and the saddened group return to the Professor's rooms, where Huxley dressed the wounds."

Viewing the game from a scientific point of view, Tait was puzzled by the anomalous behaviour of a golf ball, noting that without spin its flight was limited and that a ball's centre of gravity rarely coincided with the ball's actual centre. He stated dogmatically that the carry of a golf ball would be about 190 yards, only to have his famous golfing son, Freddie Tait, disprove the theory by driving a ball 341 yards at the thirteenth on the Old Course, the gutta having a carry of 250 yards, a nineteenth-century suggestion that Tiger Woods' length was not that special!

Right: Francis Ouimet (right) with Charles Littlefield, then President of the United States Golf Association.

The name of *Francis Ouimet* was known and respected on both sides of the Atlantic for many years. The span began at the Country Club at Brookline in 1913, when Ouimet figured in the memorable tie for the American Open with Harry Vardon and Ted Ray. The other end was St Andrews in 1951 when he was formally installed as Captain of the Royal and Ancient Golf Club. The years in between were crowded with golfing incident and achievement. Many people eyed this bespectacled American with curiosity. He did not conform to the popular conception of trans-Atlantic reaction to headline success. There was no attempt to combine the wit of a jester with the skill of a genius. Ouimet appeared more at home with English conservatism than American showmanship. Take Walter Hagen again as an example. He started as a novelty and became an institution. Ouimet began as an unknown amateur then crashed to fame overnight as Open Champion. He went on to become a senior statesman of the game.

Ouimet was a curious mixture, a bundle of extremes. Bobby Jones recorded one of their championship matches and said, "Francis was solemn as a judge, he always is in a match." The description was justified. There was always an air of solemnity about Ouimet's play. Intensely concentrated, but essentially companionable. One occasion I recall vividly. It was the interesting ceremony performed annually for many generations of the "driving into office" of the new captain of the Royal and Ancient.

Right: John Beck, non-playing captain of the victorious 1938 Walker Cup team. An immensely likeable man.

Left: Lord Wardington, as President of the Professional Golfers Association, was present at all championship and international events. He had a lifelong enthusiasm for the game.

The hour is early for all but enthusiasts. Golfers must need be abroad by seven-thirty in the morning if they wish to see all the preliminaries. On this occasion the morning was fair. It was late September at its best. An Indian summer with dew on the grass and waves breaking gently on the beach. Just before eight o'clock Francis Ouimet was escorted to the first tee by a group that included ex-captains Lord Balfour of Burleigh, Lord Simon, Lord Teviot, Sir George Cunningham, Bernard Darwin, Cyril Tolley and Roger Wethered. The ball was teed by Willie Auchterlonie, the club professional and Open Champion of 1893. The town clock struck the hour. Ouimet drove a confident ball straight down the fairway. The old fashioned cannon, shifted from the mound behind the clubhouse, was fired with a spluttering roar. The bunched caddies rushed for the ball. The one who retrieved it from the scrimmage was rewarded with a gold American five-dollar piece in lieu of the former golden sovereign. The ceremony was over. Ouimet had not only played himself into office, he had won automatically the medal presented to the Club by Queen Adelaide.

During his period as Secretary of the Royal and Ancient, *Keith Mackenzie* achieved a great deal. When he entered office in 1967, the Open Championship that year was held at Hoylake. Spectator attendance was 29,000. That figure has increased dramatically every year, now not far short of 175,000. The man behind the scenes, planning and organizing every detail, was Mackenzie. At times his views were over-dogmatic, but helped to plough up many ideas and attitudes for revaluation, forcing others to clarify their thinking. In certain respects the Royal and Ancient is ultra-conservative in the non-political sense. Only by attention to detail was Mackenzie able to cope with the commercial expansion of golf's showpiece. He learnt a great deal from the Americans during his annual trip to the States, usually coinciding with the Masters at Augusta. His enthusiasm made you forget his appearance. At times the wrinkles between the eyebrows converged in cross-roads of anxiety. When things went wrong, his face became at once accus-

Left: Lord Balfour of Burleigh (far left), whose garb became the accepted fashion norm on the links. Its sobriety was also favoured, in slightly different guise, by the Honourable Alfred Lyttleton (right).

ing and aghast like a man struck by lightning. In every respect Keith Mackenzie exercised a very healthy influence in golfing circles.

John Beck is remembered as the golfer who led the British Walker Cup team to its first-ever victory over the United States at St Andrews in 1938. The significance of that victory is lost today, but at that time Britain had never looked like winning, sometimes losing by a margin that raised doubts as to whether the one-sided contest should continue. Beck was appointed captain; whether he played or not was left to his decision, but he succeeded in welding a team drawn from all walks of life in England, Scotland and Ireland into an infectiously confident group influenced by his pugnacious cheerfulness. Ignoring popular feeling, he dropped Harry Bentley from the singles, in spite of a brilliant performance in the four-somes, in favour of Alex Kyle, who was playing below peak form. The result showed that the gamble was worthwhile.

John Beck was a first-class golfer. He won the President's Putter in 1937, the *Golf Illustrated* Gold Vase, the Berkshire Trophy (tied), the Royal St George's Challenge Cup, the Worplesdon Mixed Foursomes and other events that were more prestigious then than now. He was chosen for the 1928 Walker Cup team, elected captain of the Royal and Ancient Club in 1957. He was also an immensely popular member of the Old Carthusian team in the Halford Hewitt tournament between the wars, that annual clash between teams of Old Boys belonging to the Public Schools Golfing Society, when the links of Royal Cinque Ports and Royal St George's are overrun by some 650 golfers. Beck used to say that only by a miracle did the jamboree end on the appointed day. Without the aid of seeding, it invariably produced a worthy final, a moment he had frequently enjoyed. Another honour which delighted him was the selection of his wife, Baba, as captain of the British Curtis Cup side at Merion in 1954.

"A tolerable day, a tolerable green, a tolerable opponent supply, or ought to supply, all that any reasonable constituted human should require in the way of entertainment." So said *Arthur Balfour*. It was certainly true in his case. No mean golfer, he never missed a chance to play. His enthusiasm was infectious. It prompted the novelist G.K. Chesterton's comment: "Golf came in a rush over the Border like the blue-bonnets and grew fashionable largely because Arthur Balfour was the fashion." During his term of office as Chief Secretary for Ireland in 1887, he insisted on sampling the Irish links in spite of threats to his life after the Phoenix Park murders in 1887, and relied on the protection given by two detectives. Today's conditions might have been more expensive! Nerves were never a worry. This was evident in the photograph below showing him playing-in as Captain of the Royal and Ancient Golf Club. The ball is flighting down the first fairway of the Old Course watched by Balfour's partner, Graham Murray, the 1892 Captain, with an appreciative Old Tom Morris applauding in the background.

In appearance Arthur Balfour never varied. His taste became the golfing norm. It was always so in St Andrews. A Minute dated 4 August 1780 reads: "This day the Society took into their consideration that their golfing jackets are in bad condition and have agreed that they shall all have new ones – viz., red with yellow buttons. The under-mentioned gentlemen likewise agreed to have a uniform frock – viz., a buff colour with a red cap. The coat to be half-lapelled according to the pattern produced, the button white." The signatures were the eleven members who decked themselves in "dyed garments from Bozrah", led by the Earl of Balcarres. Four years later variations were announced, ". . . a red coat with a dark-blue velvet cape, with plain white buttons, with an embroidered club and ball of silver of each side of the cape, with two large buttons on the sleeves". Colonel R.T. Boothby, the 1921 Captain, attempted to revive the custom, advocating a plain blue coat with the club buttons, which he used to wear. All very colourful, but not as tasteful as the conservative touch of Lord Balfour which blended into the St Andrews landscape.

Left: Lord Balfour playing himself in as Captain of the Royal and Ancient Golf Club. His drive is applauded by the bearded Old Tom Morris (second from left).

Eye of the Beholder

Some time ago I was interested to note golfing reaction to a publicity gimmick that hit the headlines during the £90,000 Hennessy Ladies' Tournament at St Germain. The promoter, Lionel Provost, invited Deborah McHaffie and Tammie Green to take part, giving each a £7,500 fee plus expenses, accommodation in a luxury hotel and use of a chauffer-driven limousine. He admitted that the selection was based on their physical attraction rather than golfing skill. He did not exaggerate. Both girls were exceptionally pretty.

Reaction among the entrants was mixed. Some in trim knee-length skirts and cable-knit sweaters expressed disapproval. There was nothing personal; nobody had anything against the American girls, who apart from being extremely attractive were friendly and polite. Masculine appraisement described them as photographically over-exposed but not under-developed, with their long tanned legs an agreeable change from the usual prosaic competitors. It is dangerous ground. Ill-considered comment would rouse the ire of those ladies who are always ready to pounce on a patronizing sexist. To trade incivilities on such a subject requires a high degree of insensitivity, for feminists can be scathing.

At St Germain there was resentment that the traditions of the game were threatened by commercial operators. Any hint of imposed changes was bound to be suspect. In a permissive age, no one likes being pushed around. It is safer to let women lay down the guidelines necessary to produce a well-dressed lady golfer, and who better than Joan Rothschild to act as spokeswoman. No man would dare to do what she did. No one could accuse her of sexual bias. She admitted in 1981 to being frequently dismayed by the way

Left: Golfing fashion at the beginning of the century.

golfers are turned out. "Men dress badly, but some women are even worse. Very few seem to bother how they look on the course. They turn up in old jeans or a crushed tatty skirt that they keep only for golf. It's not good enough and doesn't happen in other sports. It does not cost a lot to dress nicely and if you are well turned out, it can boost your ego and help you to play better."

It is possible to chart how female participants became emancipated since that first British Women's Championship in 1893 was held on the Ladies' Course of the St Anne's Club. It consisted of nine holes, the double-round measuring 4,264 yards. The cause for freedom of choice was hardly helped by patronizing male attitudes that questioned whether golf was a suitable exercise for women. Their spokesman was Lord Moncrieff. He argued that 70 or 80 yards should be the average limit of a drive, "not because we doubt a lady's power to make a longer drive, but because that cannot be done without raising the club above the shoulders. We do not presume to dictate but the posture and gesture necessary for the full swing are not particularly graceful when the player is in female dress. A claim of absolute equality has yet to be made, no doubt it will not be long before such recognition is formulated." Taking a liberal view on how men had coped, the ungallant peer welcomed the introduction of ladies' links provided they were laid out on a smaller scale than the longer round and voiced no objection to ladies playing on the long course at agreed intervals when male golfers were feeding or resting. At other times "must we say it, they are in the way!" This sexist attitude was underlined in the *Golfing Annual* of last century: "The oldest ladies' club is the St Andrews Ladies Club instituted in 1869 . . . it is doubtful if any club other than the putter is used by members."

Right: Enid Wilson, tireless perfectionist, won the English Championship twice and had a hat-trick of victories in the British Championship, 1931–3. She beat Helen Hicks in the inaugural Curtis Cup match of 1932.

It has been a long struggle for women to achieve acceptance in golf, particularly when contemporary fashions made it virtually impossible to play well without incurring censure for being immodest.

In the 1890s, any lady who raised a club above her shoulder had to contend with a large hat, flowing long dress with ballooning sleeves, a couple of petticoats, combinations and a tightly-laced corset, an encasement far removed from the freedom enjoyed by the American women in the Hennessy Tournament at St Germain. In the 1870s bustles presented a problem, but nothing like the restriction of corsets which changed the entire shape of the body; such an effect was hardly surprising when a total of twenty-eight whalebones curved in at the waist.

Some combinations had daring low-cut necklines, the garment ending just below the knees. Vests had to be tucked into drawers. Skirts trailing in the damp grass were another headache, likewise controlling them in the wind. A remedy was found by attaching a leather piece to the bottom of the skirt. The length was shortened by twelve inches for playing, reverting to a more modest three inches off the ground of leaving the course. A wide elastic belt was sometimes lowered to control the wind-blown skirts and occasionally wired hems did the trick. Leg-o-mutton sleeves had to be subdued by an elastic band round the left arm, otherwise the ball could not be seen. Sailor hats looked good but were difficult to keep on. Stand-up collars and broad-striped ties became a vogue. Shoes tended to be clumsy, thick-soled and studded with nails. Coats were heavy and lined. It was nothing short of a miracle that golf was played at all. Players were far from happy and uncritical. Just as a century later, Joan Rothschild deplored the indifferent dress sense of women golfers, so in the 1890s Issette Pearson, the first honorary secretary of the newly founded Ladies Golf Union (LGU), took her stand. A dour female who tolerated little interference and described by a colleague as being as despotic as the Czar of Russia, she complained that "some women golfers bring our sex into ridicule by wearing as 'mannish' clothes as possible. They can be seen with soft hunting ties, loose red shapeless coats, and the shortest and narrowest of bicycling skirts, and a pair of thick, clumsily-made boots." Her theoretical rig-out was "a neat sailor-hat, surmounting a head beautifully coiffured, every hair of which in place at the end of a round, smart red coat, spotless linen collar and tie, ordinary tailor-made skirt, and a pair of well-made walking-boots with nails or Scafe's patent soles."

Left: Glenna Collett-Vare, America's leading woman golfer in the 1920s (centre), with daughter Vanessa and Wanda Morgan, English champion and powerful hitter of the ball.

It was put to the test in the inaugural Ladies Championship in 1893. Lady Margaret Scott, wearing leg-o-mutton sleeves, long flowing skirt, wasp waist with smart straw boater set squarely on her head with the minimum of hair showing, dominated play on the short but tricky links with rounds of 40, 41 and 42. In the final she beat a somewhat nervous Issette Pearson at the 13th after 7 up at the turn. On the score of looks, Lady Margaret must rank as one of the most attractive, photogenic of all holders on this Championship up to the present day. The margin of Lady Margaret Scott's victory reflected the power of her game. She dominated the opposition to such an extent that she won the title in the next two championships, then retired from the competitive scene. The Hazlet sisters, May and Florence, took over as the outstanding players with the same monopoly. Between 1893 and 1914, the twenty-two tournaments produced sixteen different champions, Dorothy Campbell, twice winner, became the first British woman to win the American National, achieving the double in 1909. Another name that comes to mind was Lottie Dod, a prodigy who upset the Establishment. In tennis she made her debut at Wimbledon in 1887 at the age of fifteen, won the Championship and repeated the feat every year until 1893, apart from having to scratch twice because of illness. Lottie then transferred to golf and became the only woman to take the national double of golf and tennis. Gladys Ravenscroft was the first Englishwoman to win both the British and American Championships, in 1912 and 1913.

Fashions were changing. Shorter skirts led to smarter boots that were brown or black, often laced halfway up the leg. Gaiters, made of leather or cloth, prevented sand getting into shoes. In 1909 Gladys Ravenscroft upset officialdom by playing with sleeves rolled up. After World War I there was a rash of clothes, berets and bandeaux. Cardigans had stockings to match, coats and jerseys were knitted, sometimes with unfortunate consequences as at the English Championship at Cooden Beach in 1924 when an entrant, drenched in torrential rain, found her knitted skirt not only waterlogged, but so heavy and lengthened that

Below: Lottie Dod, outstanding tennis player at Wimbledon, winning the singles title five times; international hockey player; silver medallist for archery in the 1908 Olympics; champion skater; fine athlete; prominent member of the Alpine Club; British Ladies Golf Champion in 1904.

Below: Gladys Ravenscroft (right), was the first English woman to win both British and American Championships, in 1912 and 1913. Muriel Dodd (left) held both British and Canadian titles in 1913.

she could hardly walk. She quit on the 18th green, unable to move.

It has been interesting if not educational to note how fashions have changed. Trousers were deemed as unsuitable for golf. To start with the LGU were dogmatic in opposition. When war ended, the winds of change swept through women's golf and blew away many straightlaced official cobwebs. I recall the horror of the LGU when Gloria Minoprio appeared in the English Championship dressed in black tight trousers, black polo-necked sweater, black turban, stark white make-up to protect her skin from the sun, and the innovation of only one club, a caddie carrying a cleek that was adapted for every shot. After the shock wore off, the LGU reluctantly became reconciled to such unfortunate flouting of tradition. A technical incident was puzzling. Minoprio was a somewhat strange woman. Withdrawn and reserved, her façade seemed to prevent her sitting down. Henry Longhurst, always inquisitive, invited her to join us for a drink at the bar. Her slacks were prevented from creasing by means of a tight strap under the shoes. Additional strain might have disastrous consequences.

The next shock for the LGU was the arrival of Mildred Zaharias. She came to Gullane for the 1947 British Women's Championship bringing with her a tally of fifteen tournament wins in a row. The result was never in doubt. It was like watching Nick Faldo in the Boys' Championship. Opponents were outdriven by fully 100 yards. The American's shots had the power and incisive bite of a professional. Steel-like wrists enabled her to lash the clubhead through. There was nothing pretty about the style, but the ball was there to be hit, and hit it she did with every ounce of her strength. Few women have had such powerful back and leg muscles, and that

Left: Gloria Minoprio, who shattered the equanimity of the Ladies Golf Union by entering for a championship not only dressed in black slacks – then a daring innovation – but also arriving with a single club, a cleek adapted for all emergencies.

includes that ever-consistent machine called Laura Davies. Mildred had married the well-known wrestler, George Zaharias, a real he-man. Laughing, she told me it was a fortnight before he threw her. It was hardly surprising for she was America's star girl athlete. She covered the 80 metres Olympic hurdles in 11.3 seconds, hurled a javelin 143 feet 4 inches, tossed a baseball 296 feet, high jumped 5 feet 5¾ inches, and threw the shot 39 feet ¾ inches.

The LGU had difficulty in deciding what innovations to approve. It went against the grain to be modern. Such niceties were not considered in the late 1950s when Bermuda shorts became popular. No doubt they were practical, but in appearance did little for the wearers. Sunglasses helped to soften the visual impact. Committee members raised objections and eyebrows at the mini-skirt fashion, and the LGU avoided controversy by insisting on trousers for the 1972 Curtis Cup team. They were also spared the embarrassment of seeing a team kitted out in hot pants. About that time, action was taken to foil an entrant's intention to play in an exhibition match wearing a see-through blouse and no brassière. A cover-up job was substituted.

Full emancipation was sidestepped. The rigid outlook of such stuffy views as often expressed by Doris Chambers surfaced during the 1948 Curtis Cup match. The Birkdale clubhouse and its amenities were commandeered by the ladies for the duration of the contest. Male members became second-class citi-

zens. When I arrived I went into the lavatories only to find that the stalls had been draped with Union Jacks to shield them from the gaze of women competitors. In too much of a hurry, I upset the arrangements, confessing afterwards to Miss MacFarlane, the martinet LGU president, that it was the first time I had lowered the Union Jack to half-mast to spend a penny!

Returning to Mildred Zaharias, in America she was involved in the formation of the Women's Professional Golf Association tour, dominated it and won four All-American Opens. The impact of this experiment was felt when a team of American women professionals under the managership of Fred Corcoran, one-time United States PGA Tournament director and manager of Walter Hagen, made a successful tour of the British Isles. The idea caught on. A similar tour was planned in 1979. Early progress was due to the vision and energy of its tournament director, Barry Edwards and his wife Carole, but they had headaches. The idea of women golf professionals was not new to England. Fifty years earlier Poppy Wingate had been assistant to

Left: Unique Mildred "Babe" Zaharias. A superb athlete, she won a record five gold medals at the 1932 Los Angeles Olympic Games before turning to golf. She dominated the WPGA and later the LPGA until illness shortened her career in the mid-1950s.

Right: French golfing sisters, the Vicomtesse de Saint Sauveur, British champion in 1950, and Sonia Eloy.

Left: Diana Fishwick (near right), champion in 1930. The background scoreboard recalls many other well-known players.

her brother Syd, the Temple Newsham professional, and had played against male professionals in the *Yorkshire Evening News* tournament.

Barry's female professionals were more ambitious, though some mistook appetite for ability when it came to shot-making. In appearance they merited the criticisms voiced by the redoubtable Joan Rothschild. She argued that women competitors shambled round in shapeless clothes and argued against appearing on the links looking like a sack of potatoes just because the sun wasn't shining. Her feelings were summarized neatly. "We feel that the Avia Watches event sets the style for the season and players must consciously make themselves smart." Avia's contribution was to provide special thermal underwear so that only skirts and well-cut slacks need to be worn as the players would still be warm. The practical advice was heeded. All 315 competitors were kitted out with sets of thermal underwear plus vouchers for free hair-dos. The inevitable Rothschild postscript: "If you look good, you feel good and start two up on your opponent." The ploy appeared to work. Women professionals began to look reasonably smart, while playing standards improved considerably. One last reference to the Avia experiment. Their panel awarded one entrant, who shall be nameless, half a point out of ten. Significantly, all the judges were men. It is tempting to speculate what the markings would be like if a panel of females passed judgement on men's garb.

These experiments recall some of the creations of Teddy Tinling, the man who revolutionized women's tennis gear and was famous for designing the gold-laced panties worn under a satin-rimmed jersey dress by the American "Gorgeous" Gussie Moran. Tinling was a remarkable personality. Extrovert and unpredictable, he thrived on publicity. I always enjoyed his waspish, almost outrageous wit. Over six feet tall, sun-tanned, completely bald, usually in colourful clothes, with an earring in his left ear, bracelets on wrist, he epitomized the pre-war gilded lifestyle. In the world of *haute couture*, he introduced exciting innovations that stimulated the Wimbledon scene. No fewer than sixteen Wimbledon champions wore his creations. He once said that he gave the players what they rarely had in

their sporting lives – the chance to look beautiful on court, the chance to feel like women and win at the same time.

Tinling's designing years coincided with the urge for freedom of expression. Provocative, scantily dressed young women appeared on the courts revealing muscular brown legs and thighs. The standard of play improved, spectators were titillated. He designed "new look" dresses with coloured hems for Joy Gannon and Betty Hilton and always accepted the dress code at Wimbledon. Tennis clothes had to be predominantly white, officially two-thirds white to be precise. At times he was almost prudish and did not approve the white body-moulding cat suit worn by the American, Anne White. It was officially called out for being too blatant a publicity stunt and off-putting for her opponent, Pam Shriver. It would be true to say that Tinling put sex into tennis. Away from Wimbledon, he was more daring and once put Rosie Casals into black sequins for the American Virginia Slims tournaments in the mid-1970s. He later softened his style, reverting to pale colours and much more white.

He tried to do for golf what he had achieved for tennis, but had to admit defeat. In 1954, he designed the uniform for the British Curtis Cup team. It was hardly a success. In nondescript fashion, the girls looked smart, but lacked the charismatic touch of the Centre Court. He once told me that it was all very well for critics to say that he made girls look the way men wanted them to look. His golfing efforts fell short of such an ambition. What he produced was neither demure nor outrageous. It was dull and ordinary. It puzzled and annoyed him. The girls were pretty enough, but somehow clubhouse convention had an ossified outlook. They

Left and right: Molly Gourlay, twice English champion and leading LGU figure. A group of competitors in the 1951 Ladies Championship at Broadstairs, Kent (right).

were simply reluctant to appear in clothes which were out of the ordinary.

Teddy Tinling died in Cambridge in 1991. His enthusiasm never dimmed and he was looking forward to celebrating his eightieth birthday at Wimbledon and talked of toying with prototype designs to improve women's image on the golf links, possibly getting away from his argument that only two colours should be used – as he did with the Curtis Cup uniforms – and his preference for skirts rather than trousers. He consoled himself with the thought that maybe the fault lay with the ladies themselves.

Some time ago I lunched with Sir Hardy Amies, the Queen's dress designer. He was not particularly interested in designing for sportswomen. We dined in Buck's Club, but what he said had an appropriate application. What was all right in Paris would not go down in Mayfair, and what was smart in Mayfair would be unsuitable in Bolton, emphasizing that, while a French woman liked to be a sexy lady, a British woman did not think a lady should be sexy. In some golfing circles smart clothes are suspect. In the throes of self-emancipation, which is running strong at the moment, the extraordinary ambition is conceived that a woman must look like and act like a man, the underlying theme appearing to be that though she must not show, she can suggest. The result is a mismatch not unlike Joan Rothschild's descriptions.

Tinling maintained that women's golfing clothes should in design incorporate comfort and glamour. I would add that an in-built casual touch would be nice, but it does not happen by choice. I saw an example of this calculated informality when Peter Blake brought Steinlager 2 into St Catherine's Dock by London's Tower Bridge after winning the 32,000 mile Ocean Race. The ketch looked immaculate, so much so that the film crew had to leave their shoes on the dockside before going abroad, but it was his blonde wife, Pippa, who caught the eye in casual yachting clothes that impressed by their very simplicity. That sort of touch would be welcome on the fairways. It has been a long struggle for women to achieve acceptance in golf; it has been a gradual development. Every decade has seen improvements in playing excellence and public recognition. There is still room for change in the search for the ideal golf garb that would be smart and practical with a touch of glamour. Teddy Tinling might have done it. Instead we wait for an imaginative designer to find the answer.

5
Physical Handicaps – Unorthodox Styles

In one of the most inspiring Grand National results, the British jockey Bob Champion not only brought Aldaniti into the winning circle, he gave the world an outstanding example of how sheer courage can overcome insuperable odds. At one stage he was given a maximum of eight months to live but he came back from the cancer ward, emaciated from the treatment yet determined to realize the dream of riding Aldaniti in the Grand National. Those who knew Champion felt it was wishful thinking that kept him alive. Unbelievably he gradually rebuilt his strength. He scaled his mountain, rode a brilliant race with a strong, heavy horse that tested the rider's stamina and held off the gallant challenge of the favourite, Spartan Missile. Champion's victory brought an emotional response seldom seen in sporting events. There were tears of purest joy. His example helped many men and woman involved in other activities who suffer from physical handicaps. Golf comes into this category.

Ken Venturi is but one example. His record shows ten American tournament victories. Twice he narrowly missed the Masters. Then came a slump. Three years without a single win. His winnings dwindled to a trickle. The primary cause was a damaged nerve in his back that almost paralysed his right side. When he rejoined the tournament circuit his fluent swing had gone. He could not get his right hand up in the backswing; modifications did not work. It seemed his golfing career had ended. Analysis of his swing showed a tendency to steer the ball instead of sweeping through. With endless patience Venturi remodelled his swing. Looking at it, he appeared to have strengthened

Right: Ed Furgol. In spite of a shattered left elbow and withered arm, he won the United States Open by one stroke from Gene Littler at Springfield in 1954.

his left wrist by shifting the left hand more to the left in the grip while his right-hand fingers were more prominent on the shaft. This cut out any tendency of the left wrist to collapse at impact. Another noticeable feature came after impact when the back of his left hand was kept longer facing the line of flight. This kept the clubface open and induced a fade. Gradually confidence returned. Gone was the unwanted hook. A magic touch on the greens worked like a charm. The rebuilt swing earned Venturi victories in two tournaments and the American Open Championship. A new complication was circulatory trouble in his hands. Again stubborn determination overcame the handicap sufficiently to justify inclusion in the American Ryder Cup team.

Gary Player is another example of a man who has come through major surgery and regained strength and stamina. Now in the veteran class, Gary's physical fitness proves what can be achieved when intelligent patience is exercised. When Player hits a ball every part of his body plays its part. The strength of his

Below: Harry Bradshaw had an unusual grip, a relic of the days when he played hurley. He held the club the reverse way, with the right hand at the top of the shaft.

Left: James Bruen's swing contradicted orthodox teaching yet consistently produced brilliant results.

hands is impressive. Intensive exercise helped. Every day he did about seventy finger-tip push-ups. Over a period of time, hands, wrists, arms and shoulders were strengthened. Deep knee-bends tuned up his legs. Eighteen months of this exercise put 1½ inches on thigh-muscle girth. Sit-up exercises developed stomach muscles. Today Gary is still in magnificent shape. The mental approach was very important. Some years ago Gary gave me a slim book he had written – *Positive Thinking* – in which he tells how a traumatic set-back was overcome. The theme has helped many people to cope with post-surgery problems.

A recent example of a player's struggle to regain fitness is Jose-Maria Olazabal, the former Masters champion. A long and painful absence from the game has come to an end. Conventional methods of treatment to his severely arthritic feet failed. He turned to a cure offered by a German consultant who treats Bayern Munich football team and other leading sportsmen. He recommended a course of treatment which involved Olazabal walking barefoot for two miles a day in the surf near his home in Basque country in Northeast Spain. It worked. Instead of the possibility of never again playing professional golf, the Spaniard was back in contention in 1997.

A classic example of how physical disability can be adapted is provided by Ed Furgol. A withered and locked left arm would make golf difficult if not impossible. To counter this handicap he adapted his swing, ignored the straight left arm theory and went on to win the American Open Championship in 1954. It defies purists but works. Even blindness can be overcome. I recall watching Charles Tooth, president of the Canadian Blind Golfers' Association, playing over nine holes at Mere Country Club. His partner was a professional who explained each hole and set his stance. Tooth's average drive was 150 yards. On the greens he felt the turf and paced the distance. He sank one putt of 10 yards. He said his affliction had made his hands doubly sensitive. He played by "feel". He could not check backswing, pivot or follow-through. All he could do was "feel" the shot. Once the grip was right and his hands felt right, he played the shot. Certainly his stroke-play looked convincing. Those nine holes at Mere were done in 66 strokes.

Left: Claude Harmon used the "shuttest of shut faces". Few players in first-class golf have used such a phenomenal action. The reason is simple. Not many players are strong enough to withstand the strain imposed by the left wrist action and interlocking grip.

Right: Gary Player (right) with fellow South African Harold Henning, also a winner of their Open.

Group-Captain Douglas Bader was another who demonstrated what can be achieved in spite of daunting physical disability. Golf was his game. He became a useful player of infectious optimism and an active member of the RAF Golf Association. His enthusiasm never waned. Shortly before his death, he played against Henry Cotton at Walton Heath. I deliberately say he played *against* rather than with Cotton. In that spirit he competed. I recall with affection and admiration that stocky figure, pipe clenched between teeth, convinced that obstacles were meant to be surmounted. He had a short fuse and was prone to irritable outbursts. I remember a dinner party in the Dorchester when it soon became apparent that he had fallen out with his wife. Conversation was tricky. He addressed his wife through me. She replied via my wife. Communication lines became so tangled that peace was restored. At least until the last course.

Below: Group-Captain Douglas Bader, who played golf competitively in spite of having both legs amputated.

Below: Brigadier-General A.C. Critchley (right) did not allow the later affliction of blindness to curtail golfing activities.

6
Vignettes of Fame

Right: Frank Stranahan is the only player to have won all the major Amateur Championships in the world, to which he added the French, Italian and Portuguese titles.

The value of adopting a set drill of pre-stance actions cannot be overstressed. To the onlooker they may seem so much waste of time. On the contrary, an automatic routine creates a sense of rhythmic purpose. It helps to co-ordinate mind and muscle, mentally shaping and playing the shot before actually squaring up to the ball. *Frank Stranahan* had the temperament to adopt such a set pattern. At his peak he personified ruthless determination, a quality that sometimes led to misunderstandings. Admired by many, criticized by others, censured by a few, the American mirrored the maxim that you should never trust the collective wisdom of individual ignorance. Here was a young man with the self-assurance of a veteran sauntering with supreme indifference through life with a golf club in his hand. Like Mr Pitt, he took the line, "the atrocious crime of being a young man I shall neither attempt to palliate nor deny." He treated his youth and strength as talismans of success. There was nothing wrong in that attitude.

I did not profess to understand his extraordinary devotion to the game. I have never seen any man spend so many hours, day after day, hitting golf balls into space. There was obviously some inner urge that would neither be satisfied nor stilled until the goal was reached. What that target was only Stranahan could say. I have a feeling that he wanted to emulate Bobby Jones by winning the four major titles

in the same year. He was an extraordinary golfer to study and analyse. The swing had been so regimented that the mechanism bordered upon that of an automaton. With the exception of Cotton and Faldo, no golfer in these islands, amateur or professional, and few in America, have equalled his tournament experience. I like Stranahan. I admired his single-mindedness, although I could not understand it. His success did not consist of the sum total of the number of shots he made in a year, for, whatever the sage may have said, genius is never an affair of accountancy. It was a unique ability to concentrate on a subject to the exclusion of everything else. Even off the links, the urge never left him. I remember after dinner in Claridges, London, we went up to his suite and in the sitting-room putted to an improvised ashtray hole for an hour whilst chatting on topical matters. He was also a much quieter fellow than critics would believe. After winning the British Amateur Championship at St Andrews, there were no hectic celebrations. We went to a small hotel in Elie, near St Andrews, telephoned his father in the United States and then had a quiet dinner with the championship trophy in the middle of the table.

○

Tony Lema was not an easy man to feature in an accurate pen portrait. Like Cyrano de Bergerac, the secret of his appeal lay in the fact that everything about him was somehow out of focus. The edges were blurred. He had an abrupt manner and austerity of precept, plus a characteristic American combination of shrewdness and generosity. Under pressure during a match his face became as unalterable as one of Euclid's axioms. He could be glacial rather than genial, sometimes giving the impression that the end of the world when it came would surely be announced with an American accent. On the other hand, in relaxed mood many of Lema's rounds were enlivened by the authentic echoes of his salty conversation. He talked graphically in a quiet, toneless, nasal voice. His rare golfing ability was recognized at an early stage, and I am sure never seriously doubted by himself when he compared it with others. He had an enormous belief in himself. Newspapers, radio and television gave considerable space to his many successes, but I had a feeling that what really counted was that certain people he respected took him seriously. After his victory in the 1964 Open Championship

Right: On his first trip abroad, Tony Lema won the Open, beating Jack Nicklaus at St Andrews in 1964.

Left: Alfred Padgham, phlegmatic and taciturn, dressed quietly, played a strong game, irons with knife-like precision. His golden year was 1936 when he won almost every tournament, finishing with the Open title.

Above: Arthur Havers won the Open at Troon in 1923. It was to be eleven years before another British player won the Open.

at St Andrews, he accepted the fact that supreme golfing honours had come his way. There would have been many more had he not died tragically in an air crash. He was sadly missed. There was no visible arrogance in him, no mock modesty. His ability was great, his application monumental

○

Arthur Havers' 1923 Open Championship win was a landmark in the history of this event for it halted the all-conquering Americans. At the time a home win was hailed with relief. Little did we think it would be eleven years before another British victory. Most Opens have a fluent look about the score board. Troon was no exception. Havers led by one shot from Joe Kirkwood with Walter Hagen and Macdonald Smith bracketed together one stroke back. In the end the benign Havers carried the day by a single shot from Hagen.

○

Jimmy Demaret was born in Texas on 24 May 1910 and turned professional in 1927. He was one of the most delightful personalities to grace the American golfing scene. A warm, avuncular man; a jolly man; a genial man; a man without cant

Above: Jimmy Demaret became the first man to win the Masters three times – in 1940, 1947 and 1950.

Right: Jim Ferrier dominated the Australian amateur scene before turning professional. He was runner-up to Demaret in the 1950 Masters.

or pride; he created an ambience in which ludicrous anomalies were believable, emitting wisecracks by which he hoped to convince you that he was a simpleton. In fact, Demaret was as sharp as a tack. He was a wit as only an American can be witty. With his friend, Bing Crosby, they made a first-class team, both vocal and golf-wise.

Demaret's record was a graph of his skill. He made three Ryder Cup appearances and figured in the American World Cup winning team of 1961. He won the Argentine Open Championship in 1941 and was leading money winner in 1947, but it was at Augusta that he excelled three times. In 1940 he proved that Snead was not the only Texan to win the Masters. The entry attracted every player of note, including Demaret, who was bound to be noticed in flamboyant clothes of rainbow hues and high-heeled Texan boots that he wore off the course. This happy-go-lucky approach was rewarded with an opening round of 67, later eclipsed by Mangrum's sensational 64. In the end, Demaret's consistency won the event by four strokes. Then, as sometimes happens, form deserted him. His name no longer appeared in the stake-money table. 1947 saw the winning streak return. He won the Masters by two shots from Nelson and Stranahan and gladdened the scene with an ensemble of canary yellow. In 1950 the performance was repeated, this time two strokes better than Jim Ferrier and acknowledged applause at the prize-giving ceremony by crooning a song into the microphone in the Crosby tradition. In every way Jimmy Demaret was a tonic off and on the fairways.

○

Above: Lawson Little was all-conquering as an amateur but did not reach the same heights as a professional. He won the US Open in 1940, beating Gene Sarazen in the play-off.

Right: For ten years, throughout most of the 1950s, Peter Thomson was the man to beat. He won the Open in 1954, 1955 and 1956.

Left: Kel Nagle, another Australian, was a tough man to beat. He took the Open in 1960, beating Arnold Palmer at St Andrews.

Lawson Little was born in Fort Adams, Newport, in June 1910. His golf record was outstanding. In 1934 and 1935 he achieved a remarkable double by winning the Amateur Championship and the American Amateur Championships. In the 1934 final at Prestwick he created a record victory in the history of the Amateur Championship by beating James Wallace 14 up and 13. He turned professional in 1936. In 1940 he won the American Open Championship. I can still recall Little's first round on the final day at Prestwick in 1934. His extraordinary score which made him 12 up at lunch deserves to be recorded:

    Out   4 3 3 4 3 3 5 4 4 – 33
    Home   4 3 5 4 3 4 3 4 3 – 33

As a stylist, Lawson Little had many admirers. He combined tremendous power in the long game with delicacy of touch around the greens.

○

Peter Thomson earmarked the Open Championship to such an extent that for some eight years it became academic who would be runner-up. Only on three occasions did he finish second, in 1952, 1953 (he tied with three others) and 1957; the other five events saw him take the title. A similar feeling prevailed in New Zealand and Australia; in fact, wherever he competed around the world the result was inevitable. Again he was a one-off. He was not the expected aggressive, rough-tongued Australian, but a quiet, good-natured fellow. Shot-making was made to look easy; he was an orthodox stylist who could be copied by anyone with impunity.

Kel Nagle was more in the Australian image, but was unassuming. He reserved his slot in history by winning the Centenary Open Championship on the Old Course at St Andrews. It produced a tense final involving Arnold Palmer, then US Open champion, Roberto DeVicenzo and Nagle. Palmer's greater experience was expected to tip the scales, but it was Nagle who stood on the eighteenth green needing two shots to win from three feet. He needed both, but the title was his. Afterwards he paid tribute to his fellow-countryman, Peter Thomson, for the tactical coaching he had received on mastering the Old Course. Nagle was a receptive pupil. He was also an excellent ambassador for his country. I must also mention *Norman von Nida*, a tough, half-pint sized Australian with an outsize personality whose appearance in tournaments was both profitable and spectacular. He won the Australian Open three times and the Australian PGA title four times. He was always box-office material. Never pulled his punches and had a caustic tongue. An incident with Henry Ransom, the US Ryder Cup player, flared into a fisticuff brawl during the Lower Rio Grande Valley Open in 1948. For once the Australian was blameless. Ransom was disqualified from the event. David Graham and Greg Norman have cause to praise his coaching skill. Both men benefitted. Another formidable Australian, *Jim Ferrier*, dominated the amateur scene for many years. He won the amateur title four times and the Australian Open twice as an amateur. At St Andrews in 1936 he became the first Australian to reach the final of the British Amateur Championship. It was the first time I

Left: Norman von Nida
was aggressive, tough
and controversial but
off the links a much
warmer character.

had seen Ferrier in action. Clearly he was a force to respect. Occasionally his form was brilliant, though his style was somewhat spoilt by an untidy finish. I found later that a weakness in his left leg was the cause. Against Hector Thomson he alternated between inspired play and careless mistakes that unquestionably cost the match. At the home hole the Australian played the odd to the back of the green. The Scot played a pitch-and-run stone dead and that completed the proceedings. Ferrier turned professional in 1940 and joined the American circuit with no real impact. His twenty-one wins included the US PGA in 1947, beating Chick Harbert in the final, and he came second to Jimmy Demaret in the 1950 Masters. He was successful, but somehow did not realize his full potential.

○

It is difficult to realize that generations of golfers have arisen that know little or nothing about *Pamela Barton*. She is only a name in the record books, yet ranks among the greatest of women golfers. Few have matched her shot-making ability. I remember her first appearance in the British Ladies' Championship. She was seventeen. Qualifying comfortably, she met Aline de Gunsbourg, the long-driving French Close champion, in the second round. The English girl's long, raking drives, turned the scales. Semi-gale force winds swept across the exposed Porthcawl links, but did not stop her progress into the final to meet the experienced Scot Helen Holm. A spirited start saw Pam 3 up at the tenth. It was a different story after lunch. Consistent play – level four's for thirteen holes – and the Scottish player won by the decisive margin of 6 and 5.

Right: Pamela Barton was the last British golfer to win the American Women's Amateur Championship. She is seen here with her dog, Niblick.

The next year the Championship was held at Newcastle, Co. Down. Pamela's progress was impressive. In the semi-final her opponent was sister Mervyn, who could not match the power game. The final was a repetition of Porthcawl. Wanda Morgan took the title. Then came Pamela's finest season. The Championship went to Southport and Ainsdale with a strong field including the entire American Curtis Cup team. On the way to the final her victims included Diana Plumpton, Jessie Firth, Charlotte Glutting, Dorit Wilkins and Kathleen Garnham with Bridget Newell in the final. A bitterly cold wind swept across the fairways but did not affect Pamela's game. Gaining the lead at the third hole, she never lost it. The winning margin was 7 and 5.

Later that year she achieved the double by winning the American Ladies Championship at Canoe Brook. It was a significant success. I quote an extract from the *New Yorker* to give current reactions: "On the golf course, Pamela Barton differs in two respects from most women golfers we have seen. She putts better and has more poise. The explanation of her putting is simple enough. She practises for an hour or so before every round. The explanation of her poise is a trifle less obvious and probably more important. Most of our women golfers are considerably more intense than their male colleagues. Pamela Barton, like other great English women players such as Enid Wilson and Joyce Wethered, not only does not appear to consider the game a matter of life and death, but often gives the impression that she does not care much whether she wins or loses. The truth of the matter is that, whilst winning is doubtless just as important to British competitors as it is to Americans, it is important in a different way. The difference remains indefinable. Nevertheless it exists. It is part of the national character, and it may explain why Miss Barton was able to smile at her appalled gallery with good humour when she missed three easy putts in a row in her match against Miss Marion Miley."

All this was true, and yet it misses out her essential nature. Pam Barton was such a natural, friendly character. Unlike many current women golfers, she was unassuming and thoughtful of others. Archie Compston, one of her teachers, paid tribute to her powers of concentration and fighting qualities. Determination to succeed was reflected in her own words: "In America in 1936 I practised five or six hours a day before the championship. First I played seven holes with two balls and that took two hours. Then I had an hour each of putting, driving and iron play. I believed that if I had kept a tally of the number of hours I have spent on golf courses, I should find that at least half had been in practice."

When the war started, Pamela enlisted in the Women's Auxiliary Air Force and was drafted on special duties. Sadly she was killed in a plane crash while off duty. She is one of the few British women golfers to be elected to the US Hall of Fame.

○

After World War I the Open Championship was dominated by the Americas, but during the years between the two world wars the pendulum swung to the Commonwealth in the persons of Peter Thomson of Australia and *Bobby Locke* of South Africa. Locke was perhaps the most exciting to watch. His four Open wins were all dramatic. At Sandwich in 1949 he tied with Harry Bradshaw and won the play-off. Had fates been kind, the title should have gone to Ireland. The next year the victory margin was two shots over Roberto DeVicenzo. Twice more the South African triumphed, each time over Thomson. His last win had the typical Locke touch. Wearing the inevitable plus fours, white cap and white shoes, the portly figure strode majestically to the last hole of the Old Course, St Andrews, savouring the luxury of needing five to win. The high approach shot finished a yard from the pin. In his career Locke holed out in one of fifteen occasions.

Left: Bobby Locke became a familiar figure in voluminous plus-fours, white cap and white shoes.

○

Byron Nelson was one of the few among outstanding contemporaries who by example showed how professional golf should develop. That reputation was not gained without struggles and disappointments. Born 4 February 1912 in Fort Worth, Texas, Nelson turned professional at twenty-one, but made no headway in his home state. He switched to the New York district, made a slight impression, but ran short of funds. On the verge of quitting, he won the Metropolitan Open Championship and collected stake-money of six hundred dollars. That success was the turning-point. He never looked back.

In 1939 Nelson won the US Open, the Western, North and South, the Vardon Trophy, and was runner-up in the PGA Championship. Prior to that he won two Masters titles. As with Richard Burton in England, the outbreak of war made benefitting from such success impossible. Even so, Nelson's reputation was established. He was among the elite to be judged on their level. Style-wise, his high-hand, one-piece swing ran counter to the classic Scottish method and was the forerunner of today's methods. Much of what Byron Nelson achieved has vanished through the sieve of memory, but he will always be remembered as the professional golfer par excellence.

○

Below: Byron Nelson, who won eleven consecutive events in 1945.

Below: Sam Snead won eighty-four official US PGA Tour events. Since 1934 his tally of tournament wins was 104.

The graceful power of *Sam Snead*'s swing had a naturalness about the action that was flawless. The initial impact came in 1936. He never looked back. He won every major championship except, ironically, the United States Open, being runner-up five times and third once. The roll included the Open Championship, three PGA titles, Canadian Open, Western Open, and three Masters. Altogether he won some 112 Open Championships and tournaments.

As a man Snead is a caricature of the true West Virginian, though I found his understated humour almost English. It moved between sharply defined monosyllables and shrewdly placed silences. He was never oleaginous. Whoever heard of a West Virginian being smug, smooth or smarmy? He was not even urbane. On the contrary he is an accomplished hand in the acerbity business. At times aspects of the golf scene have given him the bellyache. He has been honest enough to feel it, to show it, and express it. No one on the tournament circuit today can match Sam Snead's powerful presence on the fairways.

○

Right: Bob Charles of New Zealand, probably the finest left-hander in the game and winner of the Open at Royal Lytham in 1963.

Left-handed golfers often feel aggrieved. They argue that courses are laid out for right-handed players. The majority of golf architects are right-handed which affects their judgement. Such criticism is unfair. Generally speaking, a good shot is rewarded whether the player be right or left handed. Complaints of limited choice of clubs no longer apply. Likewise the assumption that golfers are instinctively right-handed. If a man has a left master-hand it is silly deliberately to transfer to the right hand. Walter Hagen, Bobby Jones and Aubrey Boomer were naturally left-handed though they played right-handed. Being ambidextrous does not mean mediocrity. *Bob Charles* shot down the argument that left-handers never win a major event. There was no doubt about Charles' victory in the 1963 Open Championship at Royal Lytham & St Anne's. It was a masterly performance by the New Zealander. I recall also that superb Formby left-hander; Ivor Thomas; "Laddie" Lucas, the fighter pilot decorated with DSO and DFC, who won the 1933 Boys Championship and played in two Walker Cup matches; and Len Nettlefold, seven times Tasmanian Amateur champion, twice Australian Amateur champion, once Tasmanian Open champion, and captain of the Australian team that visited Britain before the war. Altogether a strong case can be made for the top flight southpaw.

○

Lee Trevino has been one of the most successful professionals on the US tour. A back injury affected his swing, but not his winnings. Since he won the American Open in 1968, his tally of success was remarkably consistent. Five major championships and twenty-six international tournaments stood to his credit, plus five World Cup and five Ryder Cup appearances. He is a most unusual character. Volatile, wisecracking and unpredictable, the Mexican conceals feelings and intention with entertaining repartee, but behind the clowning is a calculating professional who follows a clear-cut shot routine. He is not a slasher. Few players have such control over their strategy, particularly the use of the fade. His style is uncomplicated, quick decision-making, little delay in playing shots with pronounced wrist-action, and, at times a sensible, effective putter.

Left: Lee Trevino can be a model of consistency. On the 1980 US Tour he had a scoring average of 69.72.

○

Henry Cotton was a man of few words on a golf course. Not for nothing did he earn the sobriquet given to him by Walter Hagen of "Concentration Henry". Few golfers have subjected themselves to such ice-cold concentrated self-discipline. Comparisons were made between Cotton and Bobby Locke in this connection. In his prime, Cotton would have made Locke, when in a serious vein, look like Danny Kaye alongside Henry Irving.

Cotton's ambition was to become the greatest golfer the game has known. To achieve such fame, shot-making had to reach a peak of automatic perfection. No golfer has come so close to co-ordination of mind and muscle. He analysed the theory of the game in every detail. It is only necessary to read the analytical theories in his books to appreciate its thoroughness. It is not out of place to record that Cotton was one of the few professionals who did write what appeared under his name. They were not to everybody's taste, but the sum total amounted to the Cotton creed. For several years we both had suites in the Dorchester Hotel. Often in the evening Henry would come down to my sitting-room and argue about golfing theories. One thing we agreed upon. It was impossible to eliminate error, plus his

Right: Style studies of Henry Cotton, superb examples of his faultless game.

temperament. Back-breaking, hand-blistering hours spent practising and experimenting were meaningless when temperamentally he rejected being an automaton. It was not that Cotton failed. No one can master automatic perfection. He came within sight of his ambition. That in itself is an experience known only to a few golfers. We are all subject to temperamental reactions. Most of us cope in privacy. Top golfers demonstrate their control or lack of control before a gallery. Few react the same to pressure. Men like Faulkner, Rees, Demaret, Trevino and Crenshaw personify colourful, volatile images. Hagen was the swashbuckling showman, Jones the model of unruffled concentration. Locke alternated, but was generally fairly placid. Cotton was not so fortunate. Such gimmicks broke concentration. In every championship, he had two opponents – the course and himself. Inevitably mental tension erupted. Misunderstandings became incidents. The public loves a mystery. It takes pleasure in analysing an individual it cannot understand. Cotton was in that category. He went a step further than the usual. Impervious to criticism, he ignored public comment. It was a strategic mistake. The public does not mind being baffled, puzzled, criticized, or libelled, but it resents being ignored. Cotton became the enigma of golf, a target for ill-timed shafts of abuse. Incident piled on incident. Individually nothing, collectively the effect was unfortunate. Throughout it all Cotton pursued his self-appointed course, but from the viewpoint of personality and shot-making ability, I rank him head and shoulders above British professionals past and present.

7

Scribes and Commentators

Bernard Darwin was born at Downe, Kent, on 7 September 1876. His first golf article appeared in the London *Times* in 1907 and he retired from that newspaper in 1953. Darwin once described writing about sport as a "job into which men drift, since no properly constituted parent would agree to his son starting his career in that way. Having tried something else which bores them they take to this thing which is lightly esteemed by the outside world but which satisfies in them some possibly childish but certainly romantic feeling." Golf jour-

nalists on the whole are realistic about their work. They have no illusions about what they are doing. They are certainly not writing for posterity. All daily writing is, or should be, ephemeral and most ephemeral of all writing on sport.

No writer can hope to claim the attention of following generations. He may be excited over a closely fought match, when his narrative reaches such a pitch that the echo lasts, but most golf reports soon cool and are read on the following day with a dulled eye and a lazy pulse. The method of description varies but most writers adopt an urbane style and conservative approach. Occasionally a journalist or television commentator displays short-comings that are more than compensated for by first-hand experience of playing top-flight golf. Sometimes a commentator likes to emulate Eliza Doolittle at Mrs Higgins' tea-party in Shaw's *Pygmalion*, and use what seems to him acceptable verbal coinage but to many viewers counterfeit jargon. There are also the miniaturists, the journalistic cobblers of facts, men who work on two planes, who see with their ears and hear with their eyes. There are readable writers who do not suffer fools gladly and are capable of making waspish remarks, and there are the types who like hobnobbing with the top players.

It is interesting sometimes to study golfing journalists, cheek by jowl, not of course to weigh one against the other, but to throw into prominence by contrast characteristic points of each, to assess originality and decide whether what is said or written is worthwhile. Over recent years there has been an increase in moon-

Left: Bernard Darwin, eminent British golf writer, described as the finest essayist since Charles Lamb. Twice semi-finalist in the Amateur Championship; won a Walker Cup singles; the grandson of Charles Darwin; refreshing radio broadcaster. His phraseology was eloquent, he avoided clichés and patronizing asides. Bernard Darwin was the ideal golf commentator.

lighting journalists – men who churn out their pieces for basic pay, but who rely increasingly on extra-mural work as golfing-managers or sponsors' men for inflated fees. No doubt it is an acceptable part of the current scene, but to my mind they are not true representative of their profession. The old-fashioned orthodox type has never lost sight of the fact that golf is only a sport and that there is a world outside it. As yet only one golfing journalist has trodden the path of eminence to the point where a jumble of facts and figures has become an established branch of literary journalism. That trail is waiting to be further blazed.

Even so the game has been well-served by many journalists of distinction. There was the methodical approach of Frank Moran, golf correspondent of *The Scotsman* from 1913 to 1964 – meticulously accurate; authoritative reporting by the likes of Pat Ward-Thomas and Peter Dobreiner; laughing rounds with Robertson-Glasgow and Patrick Campbell; old-world style of Sir Guy Campbell; painstaking reporting by Fred Pignon and Geoffrey Cousins; global coverage by Michael McDonnell, always readable and trenchant; would-be television commentators with varying degrees of appeal. Some, with ambition to succeed Henry Longhurst, cannot avoid the pitfalls of embarrassing cliches and over-familiar asides that have nothing to do with the job. The cameras are seldom kind.

Right: Horace Hutchinson, winner of the 1886 Amateur Championship at St Andrews and again at Hoylake the following year.

The best television commentator today is Alex Hay, whose style is fresh, pertinent and delivered with a Scottish lilt. His observations are a model of what the viewer requires: lucid information spiced with technical jargon and refreshingly accurate. He holds the microphone to his mouth as if it were a throat-specialist's torch. He is an invaluable interpreter and link-man.

I add three personal choices who would always figure in a final line-up. The first is Leonard Crawley, member of a remarkable sporting family. Harrow and Cambridge preserve the records of the feats of cousins and uncles. His talents as a true all-rounder were considerable without ever seeming to exhaust his resources. He gained a Blue for rackets as well as golf and cricket, won the Northern Lawn Tennis Championship partnering his uncle, earned a gold medal for ice-skating, was a fine shot and had a rare understanding of gun dogs. He possessed a driving singleness of purpose that would not let him rest until he reached his goal. Cricket was perhaps his first choice. Had he persevered, Crawley would assuredly have played for England.

As a golfer Crawley won the English Championship in 1931 and was runner-up in 1934 and 1937. Among many victories were four wins in the President's Putter, Worplesdon Mixed Foursomes three times, the Berkshire Trophy, Royal and Ancient Spring and Autumn Medals, four appearances in the Walker Cup, more than seventy home internationals for England and runner-up in the 1937

French Open Championship against a strong professional entry. One victory was missing. Crawley would have made a magnificent Amateur Champion.

With such a record it was no wonder that Crawley was such an eminent golf reporter; moreover, his style was trenchant and critical. As a man he was a curious mixture and could be charming, eccentric and absentminded. His personality did not readily project in forms of extroverted bonhomie, though at times his taste in clothes was unusual and for some reason he fancied himself in a ten-gallon Stetson. He took some understanding, rather like getting to grips with the Albert Hall. He had a wry sense of humour that could be pungent and highly personal. He was essentially an individualist, externally phlegmatic and as hard as Perspex. I remember one evening when he joined me for dinner in the Edinburgh Caledonian Hotel. Somewhat weary after covering the Open Championship at Muirfield, he ignored the menu and ordered a jug of water and a bottle of whisky, the latter being swallowed before the former. The finest tribute I can pay to his memory is that his personality is still remembered. Personifying the image of an Edwardian sportsman, he was an anachronistic legend.

Henry Longhurst was a man in a similar mould, with one exception. He had a problem after coming down from Cambridge. His taste was first-class travel but he lacked the price of the ticket. He drifted into journalism as an unpaid assistant

Below: Leonard Crawley, one of the finest all-round sportsmen. He could be irritating, bordering on the impossible, but was highly regarded. An excellent golfer, he should have been Amateur Champion.

Left: Henry Longhurst, well-known golf writer with a cutting wit. He was a professional television commentator who modelled his style and timing on that of Bernard Darwin.

to the absentee editor of *Tee Topics*, an inauspicious beginning to a brilliant career. He developed a rare talent for writing and talking brilliantly, briefly and wittily about golf. A born raconteur, he used to reminisce on the golden age of the Thirties, an era that produced such giants as Walter Hagen, Gene Sarazen and Henry Cotton. Two occasions I recall in particular. I shared a commentary with him in the upstairs room of Old Tom Morris's house overlooking the last green of the Old Course, St Andrews, as we watched, in 1938, the British team beat America for the first time in the Walker Cup; and that unforgettable day at Lindrick when, after twenty-four years of American victories, the British won the Ryder Cup, though the night before in the hotel Henry held out no hope for a home win. But it was as a commentator that he was outstanding. He knew that a golf writer, and up to a point a television commentator, is one who perceives what is happening on the course. A good journalist also notes what is *not* happening. Longhurst came under the second category, and I would add to that the name of Peter Ryde. Few correspondents understood more of the sport, few show greater care for detail, both were professionals with clear conception and great experience. I believe the ideal critic should be like a Thermos flask, suggesting the presence of heat without radiating it. Both men matched this definition, quick-witted, penetrating and always to the point. Henry Longhurst has yet to be replaced.

Right: Henry Cotton (second from right) and his wife Toots, with Roy Ulyett (second from left), the commendable cartoonist.

Peter Ryde succeeded to the post of golf correspondent of *The Times* after the death of Bernard Darwin. To have taken over from such a legend must have been a daunting prospect. Ryde's first contact with Darwin was with the Fourth Leaders, but he believes his appointment as Darwin's replacement was influenced by a habit of reporting for duty carrying, not a brief case, but a bag of clubs after playing an early round at Royal Wimbledon. Be that as it may. From 1953, Ryde was *The Times*' voice on the links. His column mirrored the man – quietly spoken, warm, even gentle in manner, but in matter abrasive. When controversial issues arose, he treated them with fairness and lack of prejudice. His retirement marked a distinct loss. He was quick-witted, penetrating and always to the point. If he was, in every sense, a practical journalist, he was even more a tactical idealist . . . a metropolitan writer with a longing for micropolitan existence.

Finally to Bernard Darwin, one of the great prose writers of the twentieth century. As golf correspondent of *The Times* he changed sports writing from a jumble of figures at the foot of a page into an established branch of literary journalism. Some time ago I received a letter in which I was asked to describe what kind of a man Darwin was. The correspondent concluded: "He must have been quite a character because older players talk so highly of him, yet I cannot find his name in the records as having won any of the major amateur events."

That correspondent was right. Darwin did not hit the headlines like many leading players who indulge in publicity managers, but for many years his pen and voice were the essence of golf while in his prime he was a player of distinction. I once tried to compose a pen portrait of him. These jottings may satisfy my enquirer. "I am at Trinity," said a Cantab. to a Londoner. "Trinity, Cambridge, or Trinity, Oxford?" asked the latter. The former, with insolent calmness, replied: "Trinity." In like fashion Darwin eyed the "other place" ever since he was *in statu pup* in 1894. He was a partisan and unashamed, particularly when it came to university golf, rugby football and the Boat Race. Some people regarded such bias as madness, but it was an honest frenzy and in your own kingdom you had the right to be made. The Darwinian Kingdom was a world on its own.

Left: Fred Corcoran (standing right) with Bob Harlow managed and promoted such professionals as Ben Hogan, Sam Snead, Byron Nelson and Jim Barnes.

Golf knew Darwin as a writer. He wrote upon the game in *The Times* for over forty years, wielding his pen with the touch of Lamb and the vividness of Hazlitt. But there was more to Darwin than his essays. Eton, Cambridge and The Temple formed his early background. In World War I he spent two and a half years at Salonica. Although a barrister and fully qualified solicitor, he found the lure of golf too strong, not only as a scribe but as a performer. He was in the England team against Scotland on eight occasions, played for England against the United States in 1922 at Long Island, was twice semi-finalist in the Amateur Championship, won the President's Putter in 1922 and the Worplesdon Mixed Foursomes in 1933 with Joyce Wethered. By any standard it was a proud record.

Every good writer tells you a great deal about himself though he writes ostensibly only about other people. Occasionally Darwin raised a corner of the curtain. In one delightful essay we were taken on a conducted tour of his small study in the house at Downe – the Kentish village which has seen the name of Darwin become great in English thought and letters – and let the walls speak for themselves. "You see what a domestic character I am," said Charles Surface as he walked into his picture room. "Here I sit of an evening surrounded by my family." The analogy was well-chosen. We could say that as the Darwinian pen moved lightly across the paper the words were read by a goodly company of the champions of the past – prize-fighters, runners, walkers, a few cricketers and a single tennis player of surpassing elegance in a frizzled white wig.

It was Stevenson who said that one of the most deeply rooted things in the English character is the love of sailors and prize-fighters. The latter were certainly held in high esteem by Darwin, so much so that his quiet enthusiasm was almost naïve. At times no one would have suspected him of ever wearing his heart on his sleeve. The polyhedral nature of that rugged organ does not lend itself readily to public exposure, but when Darwin took us into his confidence the effect was like a warm breath of the uncloved pleasures of youth. I believe that as Darwin saw this company in his mind so they lived outside, and he refused to credit that they must have changed at times after their fights and sporting triumphs into shabby suits and queasy caps. He was not alone in his fantasy; most of us have moods of nostalgia, even for those things we have loved only by hearsay.

It would not be true to say that Darwin was without his critics. A few belittled his golf writings on the grounds that his style was old-fashioned, verbose and over-burdened with quotations. The attempts of these gentlemen to express themselves as they imagine golf should appear in print often produces the type of journalism that justifies its existence by the Darwinian principle of "the survival of the vulgarest".

The charge of over-quoting was true. A writer who lards his prose with the fat of other men is a sitting target for criticism. Anyone can go to a bookshelf and write an article round a handful of saws. Darwin was not of their company. His quotations enriched the reader's mind rather than embellished his own essay. Nor did he carry a Dickens concordance in his pocket. One point always puzzled me. The editor of a national paper told me that Darwin's quotations were sometimes a headache to *The Times* subbing staff. During the heat of a championship only the beginning of a quotation, not always accurate, was written. The gaps had to be filled in by some unfortunate fellow in Printing House Square, in those days the newspaper's home. I often thought of that accusation as I watched Darwin writing his report by hand in the corner of a crowded clubhouse against a background of continuous chatter.

One of Darwin's favourite quotations was "Golf, thou art a gentle sprite, I owe thee much." The words were written by the author of *The Golfing Manual* in 1857. Over a century later we of this and earlier generations of golfers could have said to Darwin, "We owe thee much". It was a sad day when Darwin's pen was silenced.

Left: After World War I golf correspondents were adept at improvising. Facilities were primitive. Radio links, as indicated by this photograph, were just adequate.

Ghosts of
St Andrews

St Andrews is as grey and speckled as a piece of homespun tweed. The experience of exchanging St Andrews, the home of golf, for St Andrews, the ecclesiastical capital of Scotland, is like passing through gates into a rather thoughtful world of charm and still living spiritually in the eighteenth century. The candles are not burnt out. I went to the tower of St Rule and climbed the damp, spiral steps in the blackness infested by pigeons. From the lead roof I could see in the distance the Lomond Hills of Fife by Loch Leven and the Sidlaw Hills beyond Dundee. The Old Course looked painfully narrow. Below sprawled the ruined cathedral, once a jewel of pointed Gothic, now a stone skeleton with shadowy aisles and broken columns; a memorial to the iconoclastic passion of John Knox, who destroyed the fabric but left the memory of a ruined altar – an altar before which James V and Mary of Guise were married, a union that gave Mary Stuart to her people.

Left: The clubhouse of the Royal and Ancient Golf Club, St Andrews, the focal point of the game worldwide.

There below was the Haunted Tower on the Abbey Wall, the custodian of strange rumours; the Pends, originally the entrance to the priory, now dignified in decay; the grey buildings of Scotland's oldest university; streets sprinkled with students in scarlet gowns, many heading for the rough-and-ready shop that serves such excellent coffee. I thought of the Castle. If stones can retain the impress of tragedy, here is ground more cursed than the Haunted Tower. The gloom of the Bottle Dungeon almost echoes to the groans of victims. In contrast, I turned to the tiny room overlooking a peaceful garden, furnished as it must have been when Mary, Queen of Scots, weary of Court intrigue, came for rest and peace. It does not require a sensitive imagination to conceive what sad thoughts must have been released in this tiny chamber with its recessed window and enclosed little bed surmounted with a simple crucifix.

Mary Stuart is an enigma. Her portraits show that beauty of features was not her charm, yet, as a young woman, she exercised a powerful attraction over men. It would be true to say that those to whom she yielded were unworthy of her, being either vicious or weak. One fact is indisputable. Mary Stuart, Queen Regent of Scotland, was a lonely woman. Only in St Andrews did she become like any

Left: Pinnacle stone tower of St Rule's. It stands 108 feet high, with a panoramic view of the Old Course.

other young girl. The atmosphere of phantasy is still preserved, for this closet of Royal memories is now part of the library of a girls' school.

In the cathedral kirkyard are several golfing associations, two monuments being unique and symbolical. One preserves the carved bewhiskered features of Allan Robertson with the emblems of his trade as ball-maker in the town a century ago. He was the only ball-maker and had as assistants Tom Morris and Lang Willie. These three men worked in Robertson's kitchen, the finished balls being sold through a window at the back of the house by the corner of Links and Golf Place. Robertson was a rare character. Short and stocky, he was immensely proud of the fact that he had never been beaten, the inference being that he was the greatest player. Contemporaries said that the successes were due to his astute selection of inferior opponents. Maybe so, but he was no mean player. He inherited the love for the game from his father and grandfather, both of whom were ball-makers by trade.

The introduction of the gutta percha was a disaster. The feather-ball trade was the only one the town possessed, orders coming from all parts of the country and the Colonies. This can be seen from the records of Robertson's shop. In 1840

*Left: The lifelike figure of
Young Tom Morris
carved on his tombstone
by John Rhind, the
Edinburgh sculptor.*

*Above: Allan Robertson
remained unbeaten at
golf, perhaps due to
careful selection of his
opponents.*

the output was 1,021 balls; in 1841 it was 1,392; in 1844 the figure rose to 2,456. Anyone could mould a gutta percha ball, which meant that the demand for skilled craftsmen would cease. As a result Robertson and Tom Morris swore never to touch them, and it is recorded that the former used to buy all the gutta percha balls found in the whins and try to burn them. Unfortunately Morris took part in a friendly match in which these balls were used. Robertson was so annoyed that their partnership was ended and Morris opened a shop of his own, where he made both kinds of balls as well as clubs. In time Robertson found that he could make several gutta percha balls in the time it took to make one feather ball. He changed his mind and began to produce the new type ball at an amazing rate.

In death Allan Robertson is again close to his former partner. The monuments to the Morris family are a mere chip shot away. John Rhind, the Edinburgh sculptor, created a life-like figure of Young Tom Morris, showing the famous golfer addressing a ball with his favourite cleek. It is symbolic in that St Andrews is recognized throughout the world as the spiritual home and administrative capital of the royal and ancient game, and the name of Morris figures prominently in its history. Young Tom won the Championship Belt outright with three consecutive victories, and then the Championship Cup, but his life was overshadowed by the tragic death of his young wife in the Tay Bridge rail disaster. Married less than a year, Morris never fully recovered from the shock and he died in his sleep on Christmas Day in his twenty-fourth year.

The grave of his father, also Tom, rests by his feet. His impact on St Andrews was even stronger. His low-ceilinged shop is full of memories. The clubs he used, the balls he made and played with – all are there, together with the shattered pipe in its case which he broke in his fatal fall. The names of Tom Morris and St Andrews are synonymous. His influence was far-reaching. The span of his life was such that we have to go back to a day in mid-June, 1821, when Jean Morris, wife of the St Andrews letter-carrier, had a son. One of the first toys this infant received was a miniature club and ball. In due course he attended school, Tom began to learn the trade of making clubs and balls with Allan Robertson, whom in later years he partnered in many challenge matches. The rivalry in those days was fierce and large sums of money were staked on the result, yet somehow, despite four Open Championship wins, Old Tom is remembered as a patriarchal figure who presided over all golfing occasions on the Old Course.

Right: The Pends, originally the entrance to the priory, now dignified in decay.

Other cathedral graves of golfers include such men as Robert Chambers, the Playfairs, Samuel Rutherford, Andrew Lang and many others. They are part of the army of golfing pilgrims who have been attracted to St Andrews over the years. It goes back a long time. A parchment in the university library dated 1552 shows that the game was played at least a century earlier by the Water of Eden. The shrine of the patron saint of Scotland lies in Amalfi Cathedral, the relics having been placed there by Cardinal Pietro Caupana as a gift to his native town in the year 1208. But if tradition and the Aberdeen breviary are to be believed, he laid to rest only a portion of the skeleton, as a certain St Rule or St Eggulus, custodian of the relics at Patrae, received a vision in which he was instructed to take three finger bones, an arm-bone and the knee-cap of the saint and journey to the western limits of the universe and found a city in honour of the apostle.

Then follows a description of a rather curious voyage which ended at St Andrews. So successful was this venture of St Rule's that, by the time of the Norman Conquest, the shrine of St Andrews was known throughout Europe, as can be seen by the wording of the votive tablet which is alleged to have hung in the chapel in the town: "The bay and shore of the sea, though rough and boisterous, contains a most fertile country; this region, once poor, foul and desolate, is now rich, beautiful and flourishing. Hither come to pray a crowd of men from the most distant regions – the loquacious Frenchman, the war-like Roman, the Flemish weaver, the uncivilized German, the Englishman, the Saxon, the Hollander, the naked Pict, the savage Angerian and the

strangers from the Rhône and the Tiber come to seek the prayers of St Andrews."
Colourful descriptions almost reminiscent of the thousands that pour into the
town for an Open Championship.

The journey today is straightforward but visiting St Andrews in the 1850s
must have been a tedious experience. The Forth Bridge had not been built and
the golfer had to travel from Waverley to Granton, suffer a buffeting in a cock-
leshell of a boat crossing the Forth from Burntisland, sit in a cramped railway car-
riage, with changes at Ladybank and Leuchars, before the Eden came in sight.
Matches were arranged about midday inside the Union Parlour in Golf Place. The
possibilities of a luncheon interval was ignored. A tankard of beer at the Ginger-
beer Hole sufficed. The game finished in time for a customary dinner hour at five
o'clock. Equipment was primitive – clumsy-looking clubs with thick shafts and
elongated heads and feather balls. Even so, these vintage golfers managed to get
remarkable results. Samuel Messieux, a French master at Madras College, is
reputed to have driven 361 yards with a feather ball and Edward Blackwell held
the record drive with a gutta percha ball, reaching the steps at the left on the last
green, a distance of 366 yards.

This brings us to the Old Course. It was then much narrower owing to the
arrangement by which there was only one hole on each green, the same hole
being used both outward and inward. Any danger of collision was averted by
agreeing that the match first on the green should hole out before the party from
the opposite direction arrived. But, as the number of players increased, this system became impracticable. A suggested remedy was to extend the course round

Below: The ruined castle perched on a cliff with a secret passage, the gate-house and Bottle Dungeon, where the murdered Cardinal Beaton was preserved in a solution of salt.

the other side of the links, making it circular. Happily the scheme was rejected and a solution found by creating two distinct greens parallel to one another which increased the breadth of the course by two-thirds. This was the forerunner of numerous alterations, holes became changed in character and, in many instances, the only link with the old order now lies with the familiar names of holes and hazards. The sixth, for instance, known as the *Heathery*, would not be recognized by those early pioneers if they were to revisit the scene of past triumphs. In those days this green had no turf and consisted of earth, heather and shells, hence the derivation of its name *Hole o' Shell*.

The question of which is the finest hole on the Old Course is difficult to answer. Golfers of three generations ago would probably have nominated the fifth. In its original lay-out the teeing ground of the *Hole o' Cross* was such that the drive had to be placed to the right of Hell bunker, followed by a second to the closely cut grass of the *Elysian Fields*, the third crossed the troublesome *Beardies*; and the fourth had to carry a threatening bunker in front of the green. The choice today would be different. Tony Lema told me that he considered the three finest holes on the Old Course to be the eleventh, seventeenth and fourteenth. In a open vote the choice would probably be the seventeenth, or *Road Hole*, which in spite of improved clubs and balls still ranks as one of the most exacting golf holes in the world. The eighteenth green is perhaps a fitting postscript to St Andrews. The scene is so familiar to golfers. The white rails . . . men smoking an evening pipe as they watch the players trickle in . . . Old Tom Morris's low-ceilinged shop . . . and the Swilcan Bridge in the distance.

Below: Swilcan Bridge with a view of the clubhouse. The bridge has been crossed by the world's greatest golfers.

Right: Jack Nicklaus, winner of the Open at St Andrews in 1978, still has the urge to sweep aside opposition.

Every Open Championship is prefaced by predictions, predicaments, grumbles and praise. Anticipation of taming the Old Course is always high. For over a century the links has safeguarded its reputation against the best that was around at the time. Occasionally purple patches have produced sensational figures, but when the dust has settled the Old Course emerges the winner. 1978 was a good example. Conditions were ideal for low scoring. Sufficient rain had tamed the fairways and the greens had responsive surfaces. Observers predicted that the links would be taken apart by power golf. It did not turn out that way.

Wiles and traps dented many an ego. The 14th, or Long Hole In, again took its toll as Lanny Wadkins discovered. In the opening round he looked set for a useful 69 only to drive twice out of bounds. An 8 went on the card. He did the same in the second round. Arnold Palmer and Brian Barnes, in those days a possible contender, had sixes. Jack Nicklaus drove into the Beardies. The Road Hole claimed its usual quota of victims. Barnes came to the 17th in the first round 3-under par. 4 looked likely, but the putt ended in a bunker. Result a 6. Palmer, having carded 71 in the first round, reached the Road Hole 4-under. The drive let him down and was fortunate to scrape 7. He did the same in the next round and scuppered his chances. Severiano Ballesteros, after an opening 69, went out in 33, but sliced his drive at the Road Hole and had a 6. Tsuneyuki Nakajima of Japan played steadily for 70-71, then everything went to pieces at the 17th. The third shot, a putt of about 25 yards, ended in a bunker. Recovery shots were embarrassing. The ball refused to leave the sand and 9 went on the card.

The Road Hole's reputation is justified every time. On that first day not one of the 154 players managed a

birdie, while only twenty matched par. And that threat is still there. So much depends on the weather. On the final day of 1978 the wind veered completely and the Old Course problems changed. I remember how the 2nd hole was affected. Instead of a wedge for the second shot, a 3-wood became necessary. Only the strategic players coped with the change. In the end it was Jack Nicklaus who triumphed by two strokes over Simon Owen, but it was the Old Course that proved the real winner. That story has been repeated over the years. More than a century ago, 1888 to be exact, gale force winds swept across the links with arctic temperatures. Scores reflect the conditions. Willie Park, the defending champion, returned 90 in the first round, with men like Fernie having 91, Laidlay and Everard 93, Tom Morris on 94 and Willie Campbell in the lead with 84. The weather was even worse in the afternoon. Campbell slumped with 90, Park was 92, Jamie Anderson missed the century by one shot. Ben Sayers and Jack Burns tied on 172, but the result did not stand. Burns' morning round was found to be 86 not 87, which gave him the title, a commemorative medal and £8 prize money. Sayers and Anderson pooled the second and third purses of £6 and £3. Campbell received £2. Such was the simplicity of those early championships.

Right: Peter Thomson, quiet, good-humoured Australian – that in itself is a rarity – plays golf as if he enjoys it. Thomson won the Open at St Andrews in 1955, during the decade that saw his greatest triumphs.

Little is known of Jack Burns except that he was born in St Andrews in 1859, had his first golf lesson from Young Tom Morris at the age of ten, worked as a plasterer in the town, became greenkeeper and professional at Warwick Golf Club, and played in the first Open Championship held on the Old Course in 1873, finishing four shots behind the winner. Winning the Championship did not change his lifestyle. He kept to his modest ways. He returned to St Andrews and worked as a plate-layer on the railway.

The 1978 Open coincided with the announcement by the Royal and Ancient Golf Club that Jack Nicklaus had been made an honorary member, joining the Duke of Edinburgh, the Duke of Kent and former Open Champions. Arnold Palmer, Gene Sarazen, Roberto DeVicenzo, Kel Nagle and Peter Thomson, all of whom had been similarly honoured. In Nicklaus' case, the tribute was thoroughly deserved. His skill had become known to millions through the medium of television. He represented a supreme example of how golf should be played when the stakes are great. In defeat his sportsmanship was always manifest with victory accepted without undue display of feelings. This honour followed a gesture six years earlier when he received an Honorary Degree of Doctor of Law, the first time the University of St Andrews had conferred a degree for sport "in recognition of his services to the Bobby Jones Memorial Trust" set up in 1974 to establish exchange scholarships between the University of Emory in Atlanta, Georgia.

The passage of time inevitably means that the names of past Open Champions mean less and less to succeeding generations. Champions of today, because they can be seen in action, are regarded as superior to those who have gone before. Not only that, but the trappings have been revolutionized. The size, scale and presentation reflect the influence and involvement of big-time commercial interests. This veneer is misleading. Basic skills are no different. In spite of hype and extravagant claims, future Open Champions will be no better or no worse than their predecessors of many decades ago.

Left: Kel Nagle, more traditionally Australian with a pawky sense of humour.

Looking back, I think of Bobby Jones. Few among those following play in the closing years of this century will have known, seen or even be conversant with the achievements of this amateur from Atlanta, who in his prime could have given strokes to the majority of entrants. His deeds are worth repeating. He won the 1927 Open at St Andrews leading from start to finish and never looked in danger, but it was 1930 that justified the claim of ranking among the greatest golfers of all time. He won the Open Championship, the American Open Championship, the Amateur Championship and its American equivalent, plus a 13-shot margin win in a professional tournament at Augusta, and his 36-hole Walker Cup match at Sandwich. From April to September he played competitive golf in Britain and America and never finished below first place. Like Nicklaus, the Royal and Ancient Club extended honorary membership to Jones in 1956, followed by the Freedom of the Burgh of St Andrews two years later, which he received in a wheelchair because of a spinal complaint. The final touch was added after his death in 1971. The 10th hole of the Old Course was named after him.

Of former champions who won their titles at St Andrews, I think of Densmore Shute in 1933 who tied with Craig Wood, then won the play-off by five shots, a victory that partly compensated for the missed putt at Southport that cost America the Ryder Cup. In 1921, Jock Hutchison took the trophy across the Atlantic for the first time, though locals claimed he was St Andrews born and bred. A note of controversy crept in through him using a score-faced mashie to help the ball come back from a pitch. It did just that but was ruled legitimate. The incident was comparable to Tom Kidd's play in the 1873 Open, the first staged at St Andrews. He obtained a similar effect by hacking the ball with a knife to make it rough. It helped him to win the title. He must have been a busy man, caddie by day and manservant in the evening.

Right: Sam Snead. The US Open was, ironically, the one major honour to elude the West Virginian.

Bob Martin won the 1876 Open, but only by default. He tied with David Strath, but immediately lodged a protest that Strath had played to the 17th green before the players had holed out. The Royal and Ancient declared the play-off should take place. Strath appealed. He refused to compete until his case had been heard. No action was taken. Strath declined to play. Martin was declared the Champion. Strath had to be content with £5 for being runner-up. Bob Martin is forgotten, but players who find themselves trapped in the Strath bunker by the 11th green are unwittingly acknowledging the memory of this St Andrews professional who died of consumption at the age of thirty-nine.

Another St Andrews character was Old Daw, who used to push a home-made cart round the Old Course offering liquid refreshment to the golfers. His son, Jamie Anderson won three consecutive Open Championships, the last being at St Andrews in 1879. He claimed to have played a hundred consecutive shots on the Old Course without deviating from the line, which is more than can be said for the majority of entrants in the current championships. I must also mention the 1882 Champion, Bob Ferguson, who beat Tom Morris six times, the equivalent of a rookie giving the same treatment to Nicklaus. Bob Ferguson neither earned the honorary membership of the Royal and Ancient Club nor received academic honours. Instead a fountain was erected to his memory by the Musselburgh Links.

In 1891 the Open was decided for the last time over 36 holes at St Andrews and produced a champion in Hugh Kirkaldy of the early rugged school of Brusque Scottish professionals who learned their craft as caddies. No mean player, Kirkaldy carded the outward half of the Old Course in 4, 4, 4, 4, 4, 4, 3, 2, 4 – 33.

Nine months later he returned 35 out, 38 in: the 73 remained the course record until beaten by Freddie Tait.

J. H. Taylor won at St Andrews in 1895 and 1900 and always maintained that the Old Course, although tough, was a fair examination given the right temperament. That view was echoed by James Braid who triumphed in 1905 and 1910. Both wins were disrupted by appalling weather. In 1910, bunkers were flooded and greens partly submerged, but in spite of torrential rain and persistent lightning, Braid handed in a card of 77, which he used to say was his finest ever round. Unfortunately, the Old Course was deemed unplayable. The round was discarded, but Braid still went on to win.

Richard Burton was a worthy winner in 1939 but sadly never reaped the financial rewards through the break caused by the war years. Sam Snead was the first post-war Open Champion with a display of consistent golf that left him needing 7 shots to tie on the final tee. He used four of them. Watching the West Virginian that week is to recall a feast of brilliant shots. Peter Thomson's success in 1955 was almost automatic. For eight years it was anyone's guess who would be runner-up. Peter was three times. On the other five occasions he won the title. His 281 was the lowest aggregate in an Open at St Andrews, beating Jones' 1927 record by four strokes. In 1957, Bobby Locke spoilt Thomson's fun with 279, but continued the Commonwealth monopoly. Many will recall the portly South African in plus fours, white cap and white shoes ponderously walking up the 18th fairway to win the Open for the fourth time.

Kel Nagle won the Centenary Open by one shot and set up a new Old Course record by beating Locke's 1957 aggregate of 279 by one stroke. The

memory of Tony Lema is still fresh. This ambitious young American with extrovert ambitions to become a second Walter Hagen arrived in St Andrews in 1964 riding the crest of a wave, having won four of the previous five tournaments in the States, but he lacked a Major Championship. That was rectified on the Old Course. I recall the closing minutes of his St Andrews victory. A useful drive at the last hole left him 80 yards short with the Valley of Sin to clear. He played an old-fashioned, Scottish-invented run-up to four feet from the hole, sank the putt for a birdie, to become a worthy champion by a margin of five strokes, the runner-up being Nicklaus.

The 1970 Open is remembered not by a winning aggregate but a single tragic miss. The scene was the last green Doug Sanders was taking a long time to

line up a short putt that stood between him and the title. Maybe the thirty-seven year-old professional from Georgia took too long in the preparation. The ball just failed to drop, a cruel mistake that saw fortune if not fame melt away. The play-off was close, but Nicklaus won by one stroke, a title he thought was lost. Then there was the victory by the Spaniard from Santander, who had not previously appreciated the wiles of the Old Course. Severiano Ballesteros had a cavalier style with a d'Artagnan touch. He won the title but lost out against the Road Hole. Over four rounds he had three three bogeys. At least he was not alone. During that Championship only 11 birdies were carded. It was estimated that the full entry amassed a cumulative total of 355-over par. Perhaps the most tragic was the experience of Tom Watson, who was denied a third successive Open success by overdoing his approach to the Road Hole. The ball hit the green, but finished on the road after hitting the boundary wall. Watson failed to make. 1995 produced an unexpected winner in John Daly, whose previous record was hardly noted for consistency. His Sony Ranking was 109. His volatile temperament and over-publicized drink problem solved, so he claimed, by a rehabilitation programme, did not suggest champion material. Sceptics were routed. Daly tied with the colourful Costantino Rocca from Italy with aggregates of 282, then won a four-hole play off.

Left: The game was robbed of the rare talent of Tony Lema by a fatal plane crash.

It is essential to master the Old Course, at least in part, before the title can be won. Nature created the course. It evolved in its own way. However, there is no suggestion in the layout of a neat looking, well-groomed, orthodox designed course. The Old Course was shaped by natural forces that moulded such links as Aberdovey, Westward Ho!, Machrinhanish and Harlech, a process that began when the sea receded, leaving sandbanks and channels of sea water that slowly dried out. In time these ridges became wind-scarred sand dunes of marram grass while the sheltered valleys were carpeted with bent and fescue that in turn attracted colonies of rabbits, the right ingredients to anticipate a links of excellent golfing turf.

When it comes to evaluating the Old Course, I turn to the views of Tom Simpson, the doyen of golf course architecture, who at times was controversial if not reactionary. I agree with his views that the classic concept of design is based on the principles embodied in the greatest of classics, the Old Course at St Andrews. It may be too restrictive for some tastes, but few could contradict Simpson's assertion that "the vital thing about a hole is that it should either be more difficult than it looks or look more difficult than it is. It must never be what it looks." Any connoisseur of golf excellence will agree that these sentiments apply to the Old Course. Simpson used to argue that a bunker should never be sited to

Right: Doug Sanders, who missed the ultimate honour by a few inches. He lost to Jack Nicklaus in a play-off at the 1970 Open at St Andrews.

trap a bad shot. If a course had been laid out properly, the mistake finds its own punishment. I hope such sentiments are remembered by those who fall foul of the Road Hole.

On a more topical note, I hope we will be spared any American grumbles about the excessive cost of making the trip for the Open Championship. They have our sympathy. No one knows better than we do about the effects of inflation. On the other hand, if you cross the Atlantic by Concorde, patronize the top hotels, have your wife and possibly members of your family in support, the odds are that the bill at the end of the championship will be substantial. First-class life style is expensive. There is also a bonus that our American visitors do not mention. American income tax eases some of the problems by giving an expense allowance deduction for legitimate business. Whether a three and half-hour flight to nearby RAF Leuchars comes under that heading is a debatable point.

Left: Severiano Ballesteros, who has sadly lost the unerring confidence of youth, when wayward shots were rescued by phenomenal powers of recovery. Today such wildness is penalized.

9
They Also Serve...

Spectators have a habit of taking caddies for granted as anonymous figures moving about in the background. Fanny Sunesson changed all that. This Swedish girl, born in Gothenburg, grew up in the Baltic port of Karlshamn. She is the first female professional caddie and has become more recognizable than many entrants in the major championships. One of the most conscientious of bag carriers, this formidable Scandinavian has become a role model, a breath of fresh air in the old school of caddies. I remember when she caddied for Howard Clark, a Yorkshireman not always easy to please. He had no cause for complaint. This young woman in a man's world made light of lugging a 40lb bag five miles a day. It is hard work and the hours are long, but nothing ruffles her enthusiasm for the game. Playing off a handicap of five, she knows her stuff. Faldo has found her a source of encouragement when things go wrong. In that capacity she is a professional assistant. Her most useful contribution comes before any player is on

Below: A war visit to Vittel, where French girl caddies were a novelty, certainly to Alf Padgham. Not so physically endowed as Faldo's carrier, these frail young ladies shouldered the heavy bags with ease.

the course. At an early hour she arrives on the course with her wheel and charts yardages at every hole from every angle. When Faldo asks for a distance, Fanny has the answer with detailed notes. The girl in culottes more than earns her keep.

It is interesting to recall how caddies form such a part of the game's tradition. The origin of "caddie" is reasonably certain. It is derived from the French *cadet*, meaning "a little chief", and was applied to the younger sons of the French nobility. The title was conferred by the Scots upon errand boys and porters after seeing the *cadets* who came from France with Mary, Queen of Scots. Mention of these Edinburgh "cawdys" is made by Sir Walter Scott in *The Heart of Midlothian*. At first it referred to porters in general, before becoming the title of carriers of golf clubs.

Early references to the job have a surprising preoccupation with the rate of pay. Generosity was not encouraged. Household accounts of the Marquess of Montrose record that payment was made in 1628 "to the boy who carried my Lord's clubbes to the Field". On 13 April 1672 Sir John Foules of Ravelstoun paid four shillings "to the boy who carried my clubs". In Scots money this was about fourpence. The Minutes of the Royal and Ancient Golf Club, dated 27 June 1771 stated, "The captain and company agree and appoint that in time coming the caddies who carry the clubs or run before the players, or are otherwise employed by the gentlemen golfers, are to get fourpence sterling for going the length of the hole called the 'Hole of Cross', and if they go further than that hole they are to get sixpence, and no more. Any of the gentlemen transgressing this rule are to pay two pint bottles of claret at the first meeting they attend."

A Minute of the Spring Meeting of the Prestwick Golf Club in 1865 also

Left: When Sam Snead won the Open at St Andrews in 1946 his wizened caddie's local knowledge of the Old Course unquestionably helped.

contains a report made by a committee upon the disrespectful behaviour of the caddies, the recommendation being put forward that future lapses should be reported to the Keeper of Links and the culprit be either suspended or his pay reduced. A later note adds that the scale of payment to caddies of fourpence a round be strictly observed. It appears that the caddies of Blackheath prided themselves on being different to those at St Andrews and Musselburgh. Until 1869, clubs were carried by pensioners of the Royal Naval Hospital, Greenwich, in their distinctive uniform, who until 1832 had enjoyed the privilege of a beer allowance at the expense of the club. They were succeeded by a type who lounged against the clubhouse wall offering their services to the players. Although lazy in appearance, they were quite energetic. A golfer at Blackheath was considered a danger

to the public. He had to be preceded by a man bearing a red flag. This individual was the caddie whose other duties included teeing the ball, placing the driver by the side of it, then running ahead so as always to be a shot ahead.

Even before World War II, caddie payments were miserably low. As an occupation it was precarious to say the least. Mrs Worthington would certainly have been advised not to let her daughter become a caddie. Caddies had to be early at the club, which in itself did not always guarantee employment. Average pay was roughly 3*s.* 6*d.* a round, including tips. Allowing two rounds a day, this came to a total of 49*s.* a week, liable to fluctuation through weather conditions. This was hardly a living wage and at its best an uncertain form of casual employment.

A letter published in *The Times* from the Secretary of Sunningdale Golf Club showed what was being done for caddies of that Club in 1937: "our caddies' fees are 2*s.* a round on week-days and 2*s.* 6*d.* at week-ends, including booking fee. These booking fees are paid into an account, quite separate from the club's accounts, which we call the 'caddie's fund'. In the first place the caddie master's wages are paid out of this fund. We have a more or less permanent staff of about forty caddies. All these have their health and employment cards. The caddies' fund pays both employers' and employees' contributions.

"The caddies' shed is a well-built structure, containing tables, benches and a large tortoise stove, fuel for which is supplied by the caddies' fund. We have a large stock of mackintoshes, especially made for us in varying sizes, which are reinforced with leather on the left shoulder, down the left side, and under the left arm. These, of course, are the property of the club and purchased out of the caddies' fund, but a caddie may wear one home on a wet evening. A canteen is run by a local caterer, and his counter is under the same roof as the caddie-shed. Tea, coffee, hot stew, sausage rolls, cake, buns, biscuits, chocolate, cigarettes, etc., are supplied. We also run a caddies' bank. From March to October practically all the permanent caddies pay 2*s.* 6*d.* a week into the bank. To each 2*s.* 6*d.* the caddies' fund adds 10 per cent. In the winter months, when often players may be scarce owing to weather conditions, the caddie draws 10*s.* per week. If he leaves us for

Left: Similar caddie advice was heeded by Cary Middlecoff, winner and runner-up in the US Open, among other titles, in 1956 and 1957 respectively.

other employment, he can draw out his contributions with accumulations."

There were varying views at that time regarding graded payments. The category comprised the majority of caddies, who did their job, but were ill-equipped to give meaningful advice. The last group were village lads and schoolboys making extra pocket money. It was felt that caddies on the championship and tournament circuit should be paid ten shillings per round. The maximum per round for lesser graded caddies should not exceed seven shillings per round, two rounds a day yielding a weekly wage of roughly five pounds, varying by climatic conditions and the time of year. Five shillings a round was deemed adequate for the ordinary bag carrier. An adolescent's pocket money might be increased by a nominal half-crown.

Below: On the greens local knowledge is invaluable, but it must be heeded.

In spite of poor pay and irregular payment, caddying has always been popular. Equality of sexes in the job is not new. Before the last war, golf at Le Touquet was brightened when the caddie-master entrusted your clubs to a girl caddie, usually hopeless when it came to club selection, but easier on the eye than the alternative French *cadet*. It was the same at Vittel in the Vosges when I recall a friendly argument between Alfred Padgham and Dai Rees about the services of a buxom young woman. Then there was Polly Mitchell, of that golfing family so closely linked with Royal Ashdown Forest, who caddied for some forty years. Much more feminine must have been the girl caddie recalled by Bernard Darwin of the early days at Aberdovey. She conjures up a mental picture with a name such as Mary Dovina. Darwin remembered the chorus that came from the caddie shed: "Mary Dovina, your golfer wants you." I never heard such sentiments at St Andrews.

The company of ex-caddies is rich in characters, eccentrics and famous golfers. Arnold Palmer began caddying at the Layrobe Club in Pennsylvania where his father was professional and then caddie-master. Arnold was then a youngster of eleven. Francis Ouimet also had a spell. At seven he used to go to school at Putterham by way of the Country Club course at Brookline and managed to accumulate a collection of abandoned and lost guttie balls. The only thing missing was a golf club. His brother, slightly older, worked as a caddie and found a Boston storekeeper who would trade a new golf club for three dozen gutties. By such dealings the 1913 American Open Champion obtained his first mashie. In that championship win on his home course, Ouimet's caddie was ten-year-old Eddie Lowery whom I met in the fifties in San Francisco as a member of the USGA Executive Committee.

Another well-known American, Fred Corcoran, is remembered as a tournament manager to the United States PGA, founder of the Ladies' PGA, and supervisor of the American Ryder Cup teams when they played in this country in 1937 and 1953. He was identified with the Canada Cup, later the World Cup, and managed Sam Snead for some thirty years. Corcoran's link with the game began as a caddie and he created a record by being America's youngest caddie-master at twelve, admitting that he was a horribly precocious brat.

Right: Caddie advice can be invaluable.

Of the old "characters", there was Fiery, caddie to Willie Park, and Big Crauford, whose man was Ben Sayers. He could be autocratic and, when the occasion demanded, adamant about which club was to be used. Refusal to agree led to threats of downing clubs. For eccentricity none could have equalled Caddie Willie or Daft Willie Gunn, whose memory is preserved in prints on the walls of many Scottish clubhouses. His peculiarity took the form of being a human wardrobe. He wore all his clothes, suit upon suit with the sleeves cut to ease them on. The last garment was always a frayed red coat. He had four undervests, four pairs of trousers, the oldest being the last, and three bonnets sewn one within the other. He lived in a garret at Brunts-field and served as a caddie to the Royal Burgess Club. His diet was baps and milk; never a hot meal or a fire. The Society has a rare portrait of Caddie Willie, who left Edinburgh in 1820 for a visit to his native Highlands but never returned.

Right: Francis Ouimet on the way to winning the 1913 US Open at Brookline. His clubs were carried that day by ten-year-old Ed Lowery, later to become a leading player and golf legislator.

Among the many legends of caddie lore, I recall Skip Daniels who helped Walter Hagen win two Open Championships. After the 1938 victory he gave Daniels his first prize of £50. He was then about sixty, but on Hagen's suggestion switched his services to Gene Sarazen, who was fascinated by his appearance, with frayed celluloid collar, crumpled suit and old cap. The partnership had one ambition, to win the Open title. When that moment came at Princes' in 1932, Sarazen recalled the scene. "A terrific gale was blowing off the North Sea. As I was shaving I looked out of the window. The wind was whipping the sand out of the bunkers and bending the flags. Then I saw the figure in black crouched over against the wind pushing his way from green to green. It was Daniels, making sure of the position of the holes." It was a fitting end. Gene Sarazen remembered with affection the old man's final triumph.

Sir Walter Simpson had many wise observations in his golf classic, *The Art of Golf*, published last century. Some of his comments were pungent: "The player may experiment about his swing, his grip, his stance. It is only when he begins asking his caddie's advice that he is getting on dangerous ground." I am sure that Fanny Sunesson would disagree. After all, she is the first female professional caddie to share major triumphs and earn at the same time close on £2 million dragging Faldo's clubs around the world's fairways.

10

Amateur "Greats"

So often in golf, outstanding players are linked together during their spell of eminence. The triumvirate of Harry Vardon, J.H. Taylor and James Braid; the pairing of John Ball and Harold Hilton; the era of Arnold Palmer, Gary Player and Jack Nicklaus; the clashes of Bobby Jones and Walter Hagen; the list could be extended, after all "one star differeth from another star in glory". Inevitably the names of Cyril Tolley and Roger Wethered were joined together in achievement. Of Roger I have written elsewhere, but Cyril was a law unto him-

Left: The first amateur championship after World War I was won by Cyril Tolley; he narrowly beat Bob Gardner, twice US champion, with a brilliant 2 at the 37th. The opening hole at Muirfield was then a short hole.

self. Majestic and dominant, he annihilated distance with a swing of rhythm that was an aesthetic joy. He combined immense power with a delicate putting touch and free wrist action. There was about him a kingly supremacy.

Cyril Tolley was born in September 1895; served in the Royal Tank Corps from 1915 to 1919; gained the Military Cross and was taken prisoner. He learnt his golf at Eastbourne, but first came into prominence when he went up to Uni-

versity College, Oxford, in 1919. His long line of victories began in 1920, when, although out of practice, he entered for the British Amateur Championship at Muirfield and reached the final against the American, R.A. Gardner, became three up with four to play, eventually winning at the 37th with a dramatic two. From that moment he became a recognized international figure with a natural genius for the game. His successes included a further British Amateur title, but his finest victories were perhaps the French Open Championships of 1924 and 1928.

Right: Johnny Goodman, US Open Champion of 1933, the fifth and last amateur to win the event.

His own preference was 1924 when the field was exceptionally strong and included Walter Hagen and Gene Sarazen. For the first two rounds Tolley was paired with Arnaud Massey, who had tied with Vardon in the 1911 Open. The amateur made good progress, but in the fourth round Hagen showed the strength of the opposition by returning 66. Tolley still had six holes to play. The first four were carded in par figures, that left two fives needed to win. At the seventeenth (450 yards) he was short, but the run-up produced a 4, which meant 6 was needed at the eighteenth. A slice would have been out of bounds, a hook behind the orchard. He played safe with an iron from the tee, finishing 80 yards short in two. The pitch-and-run finished a foot from the pin. Four on the card and Hagen had been beaten by three strokes. Tolley used to say that this was his best performance. The winning aggregate was 290. Four years later on the same course he took the title again with 283, aided by some prodigious putts.

It would be true to say that he and Roger Wethered were the greatest golfers ever to come from one university. In Tolley's case he had about him an air of majestic confidence demonstrated in the Amateur final against Gardner. At the 37th – one-shot hole – both were on the green. The American dead. Tolley had

Right: John Ball played in the 1878 Open at the age of fourteen. In 1890 the Hoylake amateur ended the Scottish monopoly.

Left: Ronnie White, outstanding English amateur, whose time-consuming law career prevented him from winning major honours.

promised his caddie £5 if he won. After studying the line, he took a note out of his wallet, gave it to the carrier of clubs, and sank the putt.

Since the British Amateur Championship was inaugurated few golfers have won the title more than once. Of these, *John Ball* was outstanding. His first success came in 1872 when as a lad of eight years he won the Boys' Medal at Hoylake, which was open to players up to the age of fifteen. Seven years later he finished only eight strokes behind the winner of the Open, eventually becoming the first amateur to win this title. The Amateur Championship was his favourite. He won it on no fewer than eight occasions; his double victory in both Open Amateur Championships in 1890 was not equalled until Bobby Jones swept the board forty years later.

His only rival was *Harold Hilton*, whose record of winning both the Open and Amateur Championships on two occasions and the American Amateur Championship once would have made him the outstanding player of his period had it not clashed with the Ball era. I recall the last appearance of these grand old players. Both had ninety-nine matches to their credit in the championship. Everybody hoped that the sweetness of one more victory might fall to their lot in their final appearance. It was not to be. Both were defeated and, having reached the century mark, their championship careers drew to a close. Both have gone from our midst but to an older generation the mention of John Ball recalls a silent golfer with a slight stoop striding across the Hoylake links in the dusk of a summer evening followed by his wizened little caddie.

Ronnie White was claimed by many as Britain's No. 1 amateur. There were other possible claimants to the title, but on the score of his record against the

Above: Gerald Micklem in the victorious British Walker Cup team of 1938.

Americans in Walker Cup contests the ranking seemed justified. He was one of the few amateurs who, on form, could have won the Open title. I can think of only three who at that time were in that stream . . . Bobby Jones, Frank Stranahan and James Bruen. Jones accomplished the seemingly impossible by winning the Open and Amateur as well as the American Open and Amateur in the same season. He then had the good sense to retire. I am not claiming that White could have won all four, but it was within his powers to carry off the British "double".

Above: Robert Sweeny, member of the renowned World War II squad, beat Lionel Munn in the 1937 Amateur final at Sandwich by 3 and 2.

After World War I the name of *Roger Wethered* was usually linked with those of Cyril Tolley and Sir Ernest Holderness, a formidable trinity of amateur golfers. Wethered was capable of brilliant golf, as when he won the Amateur Championship at Deal in 1923, but he was liable to have spells of erratic driving. The driver was his rogue club. J.H. Taylor once remarked that, had Wethered used iron off the tees, the history of the Walker Cup matches might have been different. Taylor went even further. He said that no golfer is ever equally good with wood and iron clubs. It applied to Wethered. He hit the ball immense distances, but at times the shots were crooked, a failing that emphasized even more strongly his brilliant iron play. One mistake robbed him of a great victory. In the 1921 Open Championship at St Andrews, he incurred a penalty stroke through accidentally treading on his ball at the Long Hole In. That extra shot cost him the title. He tied with Jock Hutchinson, who won the replay.

Freddie Tait was born in Edinburgh, the third son of an Edinburgh professor of physics. He learnt his golf at St Andrews during the summers, beginning at the age of five. He used the exaggerated St Andrews swing, not the usual Fife ver-

Left: Roger Wethered, typical of the Old School style of amateur golfer.

sion but a smooth, controlled movement, though at times, as Sandy Herd once recalled, the results could be erratic, as might be expected from a golfer with a reputation for driving the ball prodigious distances. So long as it flies straight all is well, otherwise exceptional recovery powers are necessary. This proved the case for Tait, whose trouble shots must have been similar to the mammoth efforts of Ballesteros and Daly. The Scot favoured an orthodox grip with the right hand underneath the shaft and would have no truck with the overlap. Iron shots were consistently good over the whole range, a standard common to the St Andrews school, particularly with pitch-and-run shots. For putting, Tait opted for a lofted cleek partially modified by taking a stance just in front of the ball.

Above: Freddie Tait (right) twice winner of the Amateur Championship, 1896 and 1898.

Of Tait's many successes, he won virtually every important event at St Andrews. His record in the British Amateur Championship speaks for itself: in his first Amateur win he beat J.E. Laidlay, John Ball, Horace Hutchinson and Harold Hilton in the final. Throughout his competitive career he continually came up against either Ball or Hilton. The latter he invariably beat, but Ball seemed to have the edge on him, probably because the Hoylake man was just the better player. In 1892 Tait lost in the second round; in 1903 he was beaten in the semi-final by J.E. Laidlay; in 1894 again lost in the semi-final, this time against Mure Fergusson by 4 and 3; in 1895 beaten by John Ball in the semi-final 5 and 3; in 1893 accounted for Hilton in the final 8 and 7; in 1897 beaten in the third round by W. Grieg by one hole; in 1898 won the title for the second time by beating Mure Fergusson in the final by 7 and 5; in 1899 lost to John Ball in the final at the 37th. Sandy Herd used to recall several Tait occasions. One in particular was at the professional inauguration of the New Course, St Andrews, when the Club held a tournament after the 1895 Open Championship. J.H. Taylor was the winner by two strokes from Herd who had led by three shots at the end of the third round. He used to say that bad luck robbed him of the title because his last round coincided with a storm, hailstones making a nonsense of putting. Herd won the New Course event with two rounds of 86, while Tait finished first amateur on 175.

Frederick Guthrie Tait should be remembered as St Andrews' and Scotland's greatest amateur. His popularity was enormous and crowds flocked to see him play. An officer in the Black Watch, he volunteered for active service in South Africa. He was only thirty when he was killed at Koodoosberg Drift and was buried by the side of the River Riet. He achieved a great deal in a short time.

George T. Dunlap was one of the most popular Americans to invade our links. He came over in 1933 and impressed everyone with his boyish enthusiasm. He reached the semi-final of the Amateur Championship almost at a trot, only to fall to the slow, methodical play of the Hon. Michael Scott who, at fifty-five, went on to become the oldest player to win that title. This soberly dressed veteran walked quietly round the course playing shots, as Dunlap commented afterwards, as if he was engaged in a Sunday afternoon match. The Open that year was at St Andrews. Dunlap felt he could see more of the English countryside if the journey was made by road. He bought an old car for £10. He and his attractive wife, Mary, packed their luggage in our driveway, set off for Fife, had three breakdowns on the way, eventually arrived at Rusacks, and made a present of the vehicle to his caddie. Later that season Dunlap won the American Amateur Championship.

Right: Three of America's greatest golfers: from the left, Charles Coe, Bobby Jones, and Ben Hogan, 1949 US amateur champion, who trounced Rufus King in the final by 11 and 10.

Eventually he deserted golf for fishing and left his son to take up the challenge.

Scottish crowds looked upon *Robert Maxwell* as the natural successor to Freddie Tait. In his heyday, spectator reaction was unforgettable. Although this Edinburgh-born golfer was closely linked with East Lothian golf, in particular with Muirfield, with numerous Tantallon and Honourable Company medals to his name, the Old Course at St Andrews was larded by this dominant but genial giant, who had charismatic appeal. Everything about him – height, bulk and great physical strength – attracted the galleries. He knew it and warmed to the attention. Adrenalin flowed and for eight years he dominated the Scottish international scene.

It began in 1897 when he beat John Ball at the fifth extra hole in the Amateur Championship and then went on to defeat Harold Hilton – all this at the age of twenty-one. In the 1902 Open Championship which Sandy Herd won with 307 from James Braid and Harry Vardon who were bracketed together on 308, Maxwell had the impressive aggregate of 309, returning at last round of 74, possibly due to using the new Haskell ball. Maxwell was the first amateur again in the Open of 1903, the year he became Amateur Champion through beating Horace Hutchinson in the final by 7 and 5. In the 1909 Amateur Championship final, he was one down with two to play. At the seventeenth he evened the match with a three, and a four at the last hole was good enough to beat Cecil Hutchison. After that triumph Maxwell's championship career ended, although he played in one more international match the following season. He retired to enjoy his golf for, though he found the support of galleries an encouragement, he disliked the publicity that went with it.

Looking through old photographs, it is interesting to study his style. It was certainly distinctive. The clubhead followed a wide flat arc, with hands very high at the top of the swing. The left shoulder was high in the air with a rigid left arm. The backswing was short and stiff. Stance was wide, with the right shoulder well down and the right hand under the shaft while the swing was generated by a lurch. Pitch-and-run shots were executed with a niblick. Long approach shots ruled the pin. On the greens his touch was delicate. It was not everybody's style but it won medals galore and championships for Robert Maxwell.

Bobby Jones, as an amateur, bestraddled the golfing world. In one season this golfing lawyer from Atlanta, Georgia, cornered the "impregnable quadrilateral" by winning the Open at Hoylake, the American Open at Interlachen, the Amateur at St Andrews and the American Amateur at Merion. Add to this list a clear thirteen-stroke victory in an Open tournament at Augusta against a strong professional entry headed by Horton Smith and the thirty-six hole match in the Walker Cup at Sandwich. From April to September he played top-flight competitive golf in Great Britain and America and never finished below first place.

Right: Ross Somerville, first Canadian to win the US Amateur Championship in 1942. D.H.R. "Ham" Martin was his partner.

Record books show achievements but are silent about style and temperament. Bobby Jones was a paradox. Few golfers had to contend with such a fiery nature. Highly strung, the strain exacted a toll on his health, but spectators saw no sign of this inner struggle. Jones personified unruffled calm. His precision shot-making was a joy to watch. The lazy rhythm of his swing was the nearest I have seen to machine exactness. His record is a reminder to talented youngsters that the standards then were indeed high.

Those who never saw *Joe Carr* in his prime missed a great deal, for the breezy Irishman ranked among the leading amateur competitors. Everyone has

finger prints of style. Carr, like Ballesteros, had a swashbuckling reputation with immense powers of recovery. His record speaks for itself. Four times British Amateur Champion; played in every Walker Cup side from 1947 to 1965. One of his best performances was to finish second in the prestigious 1959 Dunlop Masters. Joe was an outstanding ambassador for the game. In 1961 he received the Bob Jones Award for sportsmanship given by the USGA; six years later he received the Hagen Trophy for contribution to Anglo-American goodwill. With typical Irish charm he took it all in his stride.

James Bruen hit the headlines when Irish golf was making a welcome revival at international level. The previous half-century had seen the likes of H.M.Cairnes, Lionel Munn, Charles Hazlet, J.D. McCormack, D.E.B. Soulby, John Burke, Cecil Ewing and so on. To this list was added the name of James Bruen.

The first time I saw him play was in the Boys' Championship at Birkdale in 1936. He made mincemeat of the opposition that week, beating young Innes in the final by the crushing margin of 11 and 9. Early promise was confirmed in the Walker Cup trial matches at St Andrews. This eighteen-year-old youngster played nine rounds over the Old Course and only once needed more than 71. The first round was 68. The next three cards beat Bobby Jones's record by a couple of shots. In the 1939 Open at St Andrews, Bruen was bracketed alongside Henry Cotton as joint favourite. Qualifying confirmed the rankings. Sixty-nine on the Old Course matched next day by 69 on the New. The total of 138 led the field by 4 shots. Then the sparkle disappeared; 72 ending with 76 left him equal seventh and first amateur. It was good, yet fell short of expectations.

Right: The perfect setting of an English seaside links. Joe Carr, Ronnie White and Leonard Crawley in action at Birkdale.

It is idle to speculate what might have happened had the war years not intervened. Bruen could have won both Amateur and Open Championships, but the ambition had to be there. That would have in spite of his style. It was ugly. He drove the ball prodigious distances, but excessive length without controls spells disaster. In the Amateur at Birkdale which he won in 1946, the willow scrub can be heartbreaking to wayward golfers. In Bruen's case extricating himself from unplayable lies cost three smashed clubs. I recall the 517-yards fourteenth. Torrential rain and gale-force wind, yet the Irishman found the target with two glorious shots. It was gutsy stuff. The remarkable feature was how he managed to hit the ball at all. Few men could imitate his style to advantage. The famous "loop" at the top of the backswing with right arm well away from the body and hands high was something that had to be seen to be believed. How the kink was ironed out in the downswing was a matter of speculation and high-speed photography. It contradicted orthodox teaching, yet consistently produced brilliant results. James Bruen was a law unto himself. If only his youthful enthusiasm had lasted a few more seasons.

A Matter of Taste

When Colin Snape was Secretary of the Professional Golfers Association, he had a tendency to fall out of favour with some of his colleagues, maybe in itself a compliment, for I had immense admiration for his organizing flair. When Snape said a thing would be done, there was no need to double-check. He was the personification of thoroughness. He acted as a goad in committee work, and in so doing drew attention to others' inefficiency. One of his ideas was to improve PGA members by disciplinary methods. Inevitably there was resentment. Any hint that the traditions of the game were to be altered by imposing changes was bound to be suspect. In a permissive age no one likes being pushed around. In Snape's case no words were minced. He pronounced that the image of the golf professional had to be trim, tidy and clean, which barred jeans,

Left: Rodger Davis –
neat, dapper,
sophisticated
Australian, with Neil
Coles, almost
Episcopalian in
appearance by
comparison.

long and untidy hair; even beards were discouraged. Before a tournament began, entrants had to agree to observe the regulations. Failure to do so could result in exclusion from the event. Decisions taken by the appointment committees were binding, though an appeal was allowed if twenty-eight days' notice were given beforehand to Snape. It was unusual for such a strong official line to be taken on such matters of personal preference, but the warnings had to be heeded. Slovenly, shuffling professionals had to be a thing of the past when it came to television exposure. On the whole the campaign succeeded, aided by the tendency of cer-

tain players to improve sartorially. The British Manufacturers' Association joined in by nominating their ten best-dressed men in Britain, an annual award that invariably produced a mixed bag of unexpected personalities. So far, golfers have been ignored. Maybe the PGA edict will encourage fresh claimants. In the meantime, it is interesting to cast an eye over current fairway trends. The older generation of leading players was too predictable.

The PGA was silent about moustaches. There are a few conservative specimens. A casualty was the growth cultivated by Tony Jacklin. It reflected his moods. There was the depressed moustache, the indignant moustache, the happy moustache, the guilty moustache, all readily recognizable. It must have been a family barometer. In that sense it is just as well that Nick Faldo did not qualify.

I used to think along those lines about Mark James' distinguished brush. When things did not go right or someone in the gallery was being tiresome, these characteristics became exaggerated. He looked like Dr Watson trying to do a Holmes. Malcolm Gregson was another. He favoured a combined moustache and beard outfit. It improved what otherwise was a regiment of teeth. Of the Continental moustaches, Antonio Garrido mirrored European aplomb. Even down to the smallest gesture, he was trim and well groomed. All Spanish gesticulations are variations of the shrug. Garrido even succeeded in bringing an air of fastidiousness to his expression.

Tom Watson never seems to alter. He resembled on all-American student with a casual touch of elegance and a taste in shirts which suggests a selection influenced by his wife. Nick Faldo is thoughtfully well groomed and avoids American brashness. The moustached Rodger Davis was slightly reminiscent of David Niven. On the fairways the Australian can look snazzy; at night-time in his Sunday best somewhat self-conscious, quite unlike his fellow-countrymen. Kel Nagle was more down to earth. Norman von Nida could have stepped out of *Guys and Dolls*. Peter Thomson was always bright, breezy and precise. Greg Norman favours a Runyonesque manner of dressing with a hat mercifully held up by his ears. Neil Coles has always had an episcopalian appearance as he meanders round in benign fashion looking for a biretta.

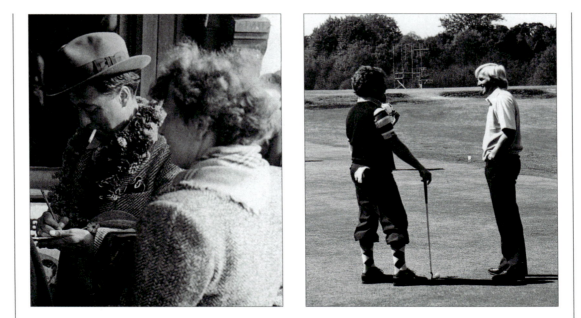

Tom Kite is not a romantic figure. At his height you cannot be; nor is he a fashion plate, but he does have plenty of natural charm behind outsize glasses. Peter Alliss has what it takes to look puffily smart, but must watch his waistline. Sam Torrance, a congenial, mischievous individual, has a permanent air of Scottish insouciance. Vincente Fernandez' eyebrows and hands are as voluble as his lips. Off the links he is slickly smart. Brian Huggett plumped for comfort rather than effect. He was an admirable ambassador for the Principality. Severiano Ballesteros has a dark Latin appearance, fine features, is rarely well tailored, but Spanish charm can get away with anything. Johnny Miller can be conservative or self-consciously extrovert. Brian Barnes could be reasonably tidy with trousers, even shorts that periodically looked too tight. He should have taken some tips from his father-in-law, the veteran Max Faulkner, who ranked as the peacock of the links. At times his colour schemes caused mental astigmatism.

But such eye-catching fashion plates seem dull compared with some of the old campaigners. I once listened to the legendary Walter Hagen talk about the psychological advantage of looking smarter than your opponent. He recalled how his competitive campaign began in 1913 when he appeared at Brookline in a pair of grey flannels, a striped silk shirt, a fancy bandana – tied cowboy fashion around the neck – and a checked Scottish cap. Of course there were the heavy-soled brogues with the wide tongue that doubled back and spread out over the instep. This was the costume *de rigueur* among the professionals at that time.

Walter had seen one big Open championship – the affair at Buffalo the year before – where he obtained some valuable pointers on sartorial art and some intimate knowledge of the field of stars against whom he was to compete in future years. At the time he was assistant to Al Christie, who was the professional at the Rochester Country Club. Walter told me how one day he had confided to the boss his intention of going over to Buffalo and playing in the Open. Al was so convincingly discouraging that he frightened him out of playing. However, there was no harm in watching the "big shots" perform so he went over to get a close up of his heroes and the more he observed their play the better he thought of himself. He returned to Rochester having determined that nothing would keep him from competing in the championship. It was a prophecy that bore fruit.

Returning to more current players, Raymond Floyd is another who never varies. Seldom ruffled, outwardly imperturbable, he paces a round to suit his mental tempo. Garb matches the man. Nothing dashing, plain, practical, with an incongruous postscript of a tartan bonnet. Bernard Gallacher tries to look neat, but does not always succeed. Lee Trevino is still the "character" of the game. Arms windmilling, he gives the impression of being possessed by an adhesive demon that is fiercely resisting exorcism. With such mannerisms, no one notices what he is wearing. Gene Littler was ultra-conservative in dress. When things were going right, he took on a protective colouring which melted him into his background like a lizard on a rock. His garments passed unnoticed, but for the opposite reason to Trevino.

Peter Oosterhuis tried to keep up with the Americans. It did not come naturally and must have been tough cultivating a carefree appearance on the American circuit when the breaks did not come. Christy O'Connor personified Irish comfort. Hale Irwin is a difficult man to describe sartorially. He has a sad, anonymous face accentuated now he has joined the veteran class. He resembles a rather severe country solicitor who might well be on the board of governors of the local hospital. His attributes make him uncontroversial.

At times Gary Player is over-severe with himself. When it comes to golf, he judges himself by self-decided standards, and the measuring-rod has been well nigh perfection. He apologizes for mistakes that in others would not be noticed. He says so much in the confessional that the priest cannot get a word in sideways. With that painstaking, methodical approach to the game, he still applies similar standards to his dress and appearance. Trim, neat, smart, functional, he always looks completely right when he stands on the tee. No flashy side effects, just good taste. . .

This list is by no means definitive. It could not be without the likes of Nicklaus, Lyle, Crenshaw, Palmer, Aoki, Stadler, Cotton, Locke, Sarazen, Hogan and Snead, but there are enough examples to indicate that the golfing world is refreshingly normal as regards sartorial standards. There are a few exceptions in both directions.

Left: The Earl of Dudley indulging in an extravagant follow-through, though where the ball finished after such a flamboyant flourish is speculative.

The trendy ones will ape the off-beat fashions until they become more mature. The hopeless ones will remain hopeless. The only consolation is that clothes by themselves prove nothing – unless you place significance on the rule of a nudist club in London which requires club servants to wear short aprons on duty so as to preserve some form of social distinction.

12
So Near...
So Far

When the dust settles after every Open Championship, the Champion's name is engraved on the trophy in time for the official presentation. Another chapter in the long history of this most coveted of championships has closed. The prestigious rota of past winners speaks for itself. Victors are remembered, their challengers forgotten. It has always been like that. It always will be. And yet, it seems unfair to forget those who missed fame through a missed putt or hesitant shot. In the majority of cases the opportunity to make amends never returns. It was their one chance to win the title and they blew it.

Right: Syd Scott, quiet, consistent, methodical.

The margin between success and failure is narrow. Contestants are evenly matched. In action, all strike the ball equally well. There is little to choose between them. Champions are not necessarily the most powerful men or the best strikers of the ball. They are not "naturals" born with the genetic gifts to win. The determining factor is often the reaction to cruel moments of tension when "yips" strike and confidence evaporates. Occasionally luck plays a big part.

Think of Roger Wethered at the 1921 Open. In the third round at St Andrews he went forward at the 14th hole to size up the second shot, stepped backwards and trod on his own ball. That penalty shot made all the difference. He tied with Jock Hutchison on 296 and lost the replay. Another controversial factor was Hutchison's controversial use of a score-faced mashie.

Twenty-eight years later in 1949 Harry Bradshaw was even more unfortunate. The scene was Sandwich, on the Kent coast. The Irishman, casually dressed, sauntered round the course completely unconcerned, playing shots without any apparent effort or worry. The attitude paid dividends. He led the qualifiers with rounds of 67 and 72, then headed the field with a first round of 68. He began the second in confident style with four fours, but drove into the rough at the 450 yard 5th. The ball finished inside a bottle. He decided to play the ball as it lay, shattered the bottle with an iron, but only made 40 yards. The incident upset the rhythm of his game. 77 ruined his chances. 68 and 70 tied with Bobby Locke on an aggregate of 283. The South African won the replay on a scorching hot day to take his first Open title. Later that season I saw the tables turned in Ireland, Bradshaw winning the Irish Open by a single stroke from Locke on the Belvoir Park course, but it was still second best.

It always seems unjust that Dai Rees was never Open Champion. Time and again the gutsy little Welshman looked like winning when a jinx struck. One of these occasions was the first Open after the war in 1948. Three rounds completed, he shared the lead with Sam Snead and Johnny Bulla and began the last round in jaunty fashion. The opening hole on the Old Course at St Andrews does not present undue problems, but his drive was wild. It went straight for the rails, struck a spectator and luckily fell a couple of feet inside the course. The reprieve was brief. The second shot went into the burn – seven on the card. Three putts at the second for a five. Twelve shots for two holes. Three putts at the third. 42 at the turn. Rees did not give up. Three at the Road Hole, four at the 18th meant 80 and aggregate of 295. Snead cruised home by four strokes.

Johnny Bulla is hardly remembered today, but the tall American could so easily have won the Open twice. In 1939 he caused quite a stir. Powerfully built with a rapid swing and a preference for drug store golf balls with no pedigree, he tackled the Old Course at St Andrews. He carded the

Right: Johnny Bulla, American who just missed out on the "Majors".

opening round with an undistinguished 77, but then had consecutive rounds of 71 ending with a 73. Dick Burton needed 72 to win. He made no mistake. 3 at the 18th clinched the title by two strokes. Jack Newton had his moment at Carnoustie in 1975. He tied with Tom Watson on 279 after several putts just missed and lost the play-off by one stroke. Tragically he could never repeat the challenge because of horrific injuries sustained in an aeroplane accident. Jack Newton would have been a popular champion.

Other first-timers include Simon Owen who in 1978 hit the headlines as an outsider with the Championship in his sights. His 3rd round of 67 on the Old Course was brilliant. The purple patch faltered on the last day but 71 was good enough to share second place, two strokes behind Jack Nicklaus. If only those early putts had dropped. The New Zealander enjoyed his moment of fame, then disappeared into obscurity. Tom Kite likewise has had his chances in the Open. The little man with the huge glasses has a style of his own that appeals to the galleries. He has skirted success. Expressions of sympathy are maybe muted slightly by the fact that he has topped the million dollar ceiling on stake money. In a way, perhaps, the pain has been eased.

Think how playing careers and bank balances might have been altered if Phil Rodgers had sunk a critical putt in the 1963 Open at Lytham. That error cost him the title. The same might be said of Dave Thomas who threw it away on the same course in 1958 by one stroke. He had his chance again eight years later at Muirfield, only to be pipped by Nicklaus by one shot. Few today realize that Thomas could have been Open Champion twice. Another upset occurred at Carnoustie in 1931 when Jose Jurado

from the Argentine had a healthy lead of three strokes after three rounds, then lost confidence on the greens. Everything turned on the closing holes. MacSmith would have won with a par finish of 3-4-5. Instead he needed 6-5-5. Tommy Armour had finished the inward half in 36 for an aggregate of 296. Jurado needed 3-4-5 for victory, but saw his hopes disappear when the tee-shot to the 17th finished in the burn. He lost by a single stroke.

In 1927 at St Andrews the title might have been won by either Aubrey Boomer or Fred Robson. Both players had impressive records. They were stylists of the Golden Age with fluent rhythm. It is sad they never again came so close to the Championship. The same might be said of Archie Compston. His physical presence was overwhelming. Over 6 foot tall, he was always exciting to watch. Galleries were attracted by the spectacle of this massive professional lashing into the ball with a fury beyond the reach of his colleagues. John Daly today makes a similar impact, though in his case there is little charisma. Compston was value for money, but good wishes do not affect the score card. He failed by one shot to win the title at Prestwick in 1925 and threw away his best chance at Hoylake in 1930. A third round of 68 put him in contention with Bobby Jones. Instead he floundered with an 82. A one-shot lead became a six-shot deficit.

Left: Jimmy Adams, flowing St Andrews swing, infectiously cheerful.

Neil Coles might have been Open Champion in 1973. It would have been a highly popular win, and a rebuff to those who were inclined, respectfully and wrongly, to dismiss him as being too old. They forgot that when natural skill and experienced determination are combined, as they were in the case of Coles, anything was possible. This avuncular professional held the gate against the younger generation. In that same championship, Johnny Miller was the threat to Tom Weiskopf but made amends by taking the title three years later at Birkdale. After that his form disappeared. Years in the wilderness followed.

Bob Charles, Open Champion of 1963, could have added the 1968 and 1969 titles to his collection had three erring putts dropped. Syd Scott came within two strokes of beating Peter Thomson in the 1954 Open. Scott was not by nature a headliner when it came to news, but always gave a workmanlike performance without showiness. He was submerged in his job. Had that one-off success happened, he might have become more ambitious. Another professional who could have registered two Open victories was Flory van Donck. The Belgian was such a seasoned campaigner that pre-war galleries expected him to do well. They were seldom disappointed. The turning-point came after just failing to beat Gary Player at Muirfield in 1959. Reaction left him a tired man.

Jimmy Adams would have been a warm-hearted champion. This burly Scot with flowing St Andrews swing and a surprisingly delicate putting touch had the ideal temperament. If only he had not faltered in the last round at Hoylake in

1936. Two fours were needed on the final two holes. Five at the Royal meant 3 at the last. It was a brave effort. The ball looked in the hole but stayed out.

That drama was eclipsed in the epic struggle at Sandwich two years later. In unbelievably bad weather with wind of gale force, the title was between Adams and Reginald Whitcombe, both giants in stature. The standard of golf was remarkably high and it was a pity that either had to lose. In the end Reginald won by two shots, and the ultimate honour had gone to a member of the Whitcombe family who tried so long to win the title, an onslaught lasting twenty years. On several occasions it was in their grasp, but each time faltered in the run-in. A few statistics confirm the point. In 1924 Ernest finished second. Charles was fourth in 1932, fifth in 1922, 1927 and 1934, third in 1935. Reginald came fifth in 1933 and second in 1937. That looked to be his year. The full strength of the American Ryder Cup team was in the field riding the crest of the wave after beating Great Britain at Southport. Carnoustie was exacting, the weather frightful, and the combination played havoc with all but the most powerful shot-makers. Reginald set a cracking pace. The Americans were jolted out of their stride. Moral victory went to Whitcombe, but in the closing stages it was Henry Cotton who took the title with some devastating golf. It seemed the Whitcombes were fated never to win the Open. Opportunity knocked once more. In spite of those gale force winds that

Below: Reginald Whitcombe with Percy Alliss (right).

Below: Ray Floyd with Dave Thomas (right).

swept across the exposed Royal St George's fairways, tearing down the huge marquee, it had little effect on Reginald's play. An opening round of 71, followed by 75 and 78, and an aggregate of 295 gave him victory by those two precious shots.

Ben Crenshaw must be the most frustrated professional of the current bunch. Few men have had such wretched luck over so long a period. Shot for shot, few can equal his skill. Lop half a dozen shots off his championship rounds and Ben would rank as one of the "greats", with the Open among his scalps. Instead he is known as the world's runner-up. Doug Sanders knew the feeling at St Andrews in 1970 when a missed putt of a few inches on the last hole lost him he title which went to Nicklaus on the replay. Frank Stranahan would have been sympathic. Hoylake 1947. Last hole of the championship. Two needed to tie. The hole is some 400 yards. The second has to carry a strategic bunker to an expansive green. The ball finished only inches from the hole. Fred Daly became champion by one shot.

The list of almost champions is lengthy. To name but a few I think of courteous Lu Liang Huan, runner-up to Lee Trevino at Birkdale in 1971. George Duncan in 1922. Al Watrous, frustrated by Bobby Jones at Lytham. His superb bunker shot at the 17th is commemorated by a bronze plate in the sand-trap. Gene Sarazen at Sandwich in 1928 when Walter Hagen beat him by two shots. Sarazen laid the blame on the long Suez Canal Hole that cost him a seven. Leo Deigel, the out-elbows putter, failed by two strokes at Hoylake in 1930. Craig Wood tied with Densmore Shute in 1933, but lost the replay. Syd Brews did his best to contain Henry Cotton at Sandwich in 1934, but failed. The phlegmatic Alfred Padgham fell four strokes short of overhauling the slash-

Right: Sam King, imperturbable, seldom showed emotion.

ing Alf Perry at Muirfield. Reg Horne might have succeeded in 1947, a win that would have transformed his career. Antonio Cerda might have held the title twice. Gordon J. Brand might have been champion in 1986. In our lives, "if" usually takes the form of "if only", and generally carries with it implications of regret. It is interesting to speculate how golfing history might have been altered had a putt not been missed. One incident can affect a player's career, an unlucky break can make the difference between fame and obscurity. Sadly in championships it is only the winner who counts. To be runner-up is gratifying, but the feat is only remembered as long as the presentation ceremony lasts. These are the men who can say with feeling, "if only . . .".

13

Ryder Cup and Masters Reflections

Samuel Ryder was an astute businessman with a flair for marketing. When he found that the family corn-chandlers set-up in Manchester had little appeal with disappointing profits, he switched from selling vegetable and flower seed by weight to the gimmick of offering smaller quantities in penny packets. The novelty caught on. Premises were obtained in St Albans, Hertfordshire, and business expanded in other channels. Ryder joined Verulam Golf Club, not so much for the game but as a means of widening his circle of contacts. The club professional, Abe Mitchell, interested him. Here was a golfer widely tipped as a future Open Champion, but frustrated in his efforts to succeed by the demands of his job that ruled out serious preparation for tournaments and championships. Ryder eased the pressure by appointing Mitchell his private coach, becoming the patron of one of the finest golfers never to win the Open title, a parallel to Sam

Right: Ed Dudley (facing the camera) had the distinction of being President of the US PGA for seven successive years, seen here at Stratford-upon-Avon. Dudley had one swing for all his clubs: always unhurried and placid.

Snead's later efforts to win the US Open title. Their records are similar in that each of them collected innumerable honours, but they both missed out on the most coveted of titles.

Abe Mitchell is but a name in the record books, a shadowy statistic that does little for his memory. He bridged two eras. His playing career went back to the heyday of John Ball and Harold Hilton, yet he played in the 1933 Ryder Cup match at Southport and Ainsdale alongside such men as Alfred Padgham, Gene Sarazen, Alfred Perry and Walter Hagen. At the outset Mitchell was a prominent member of the Cantelupe Artisan Club at Forest Row. His handicap of plus-ten spoke for itself. The potential was recognized by selection for the England side against Scotland, later reaching the semi-finals of the Amateur Championship. In 1912 Mitchell was in the Amateur final at Westward Ho!, but just missed out. Advantage off the tee gave him a 3-hole lead at the end of the first round, but he faltered after lunch. John Ball squared the match on the 33rd green. The next

Right: Charles Whitcombe, British Ryder Cup captain. Captain in the 1949 match.

hole was halved when the Hoylake player coped with a partial stymie. Mitchell won the 35th, but fluffed a short putt on the final green for match and title. 37th was halved. 38th was disastrous. Mitchell was trapped in a ditch. The recovery shot caused the ball to hit his body, that was that.

The following year saw Mitchell join the professional ranks and he finished 4th in the Open at Prestwick. War years interrupted a career that could have touched its peak in the same way that Richard Burton never capitalized on the Open win at St Andrews in 1939.

When championship golf resumed at Deal in 1920, Mitchell stormed back intent on making up for the wasted years. Opening rounds of 74 and 73 gave him a 6-stroke advantage over Sandy Herd. Things went wrong in the third round. George Duncan carded 71. Mitchell slumped to 84. Duncan added a 72 which gave him the title by two strokes from Herd. Mitchell finished with 76 for 4th place. That more or less summarizes his story. Victories denied through momentary lapses in concentration. He was a natural golfer, a long hitter who found the rough like Ballesteros in a wild mood. His rhythmic action was flawless. Long irons were slightly suspect, but meticulous approach work won many a match. Few men could so unerringly roll two shots into one. On the greens he gave the hole a chance.

Mitchell's Ryder Cup record was impressive. In the first international match between Great Britain and the United States promoted by the *Glasgow Herald* at Gleneagles in 1921, he was paired with George Duncan, halved the foursome against Jock Hutchison and Walter Hagen and did the same against Hagen in the singles. The match was repeated at Wentworth in 1926. This time the same pair outclassed Hagen and Jim Barnes by 9 and 8, then beat Barnes in the singles by 8 and 7. In 1929 Mitchell teamed with Fred Robson to beat Gene Sarazen and Ed

Dudley 2 and 1, but lost to Leo Diegel 9 and 8. Scioto in 1931 saw Mitchell again paired with Robson. They played well to beat Diegel and Al Espinosa 2 and 1, but lost to Wiffy Cox 3 and 1. Then at Southport in 1933, Mitchell and Arthur Havers defeated Olin Dutra and Densmore Shute 3 and 1, followed by a satisfying win over Dutra by 9 and 8. That was the last match of his Ryder Cup career. Those who saw Abe Mitchell in action will recall a compact figure, neatly dressed, quiet in mannerisms, cap well over the eyes, driving the ball tremendous distances with an abbreviated follow through. He was a formidable match player who had the misfortune to clash with the Triumvirate, then had to cope with a fierce American invasion.

Returning to Sam Ryder, his incursion into the world of golf has survived the test of time. The tall, thin seed-merchant presented a gold cup in 1927 named after the donor for competition biennially between teams representing the PGA of Great Britain and the PGA of America. One of the conditions was that the teams should consist of home-bred professionals resident in their country at the time of selection. This was to prevent a repetition of what happened in the match arranged by George Duncan in 1926 at Wentworth. Tommy Armour of Scotland, Joe Kirkwood of Australia, plus Jim Barnes and Cyril Walker of England lined up in the American team. The inaugural Ryder Cup match was played at Worcester, Massachusetts, in 1927 and was an instant success. There was one snag. The trophy was not endowed. The PGA was expected to finance the event. Such worries are now a thing of the past. Revenue from television coverage, sponsors, advertising, gate money and the media have seen to that. The fact remains that Samuel Ryder has the credit for a unique commercial deal. Consider the big money spent every time by sponsors to ensure continuity of identity, Dunhills having to invest a fortune to gain entry into the golfing scene, whilst Ryder has had global publicity for some seventy years for the price of a trophy. In any language it has been a good return.

Below: The victorious 1949 US Ryder Cup team with Ben Hogan holding the gold trophy.

Left: Outside Christ Church, Oxford. Sam Snead (far right) surveys the scene with folded arms and talks to Dutch Harrison. Ben Hogan is in the centre group.

Right: Facing probable defeat in the 1957 Ryder Cup, the Americans Fred Hawkins, Doug Ford and Art Wall looking anxiously glum.

But there was more to it than brass. Sam Ryder was rightly proud of this event based on Anglo-American rivalry. He used to say that genuine goodwill had been promoted between players and the public on both sides of the Atlantic. It was a team effort on a national basis and stake money was not all-important for a change; good traditional stuff, match-play duels between the finest golfers of two nations. At times the matches were one-sided, but when I asked him if he thought the basis of selection should be widened to include other nationalities, he dismissed the thought as unacceptable. If that ever happened he felt it would cease to be the Ryder Cup match as laid down in the initial conditions of acceptance. A European line-out would become just another vamped-up tournament, a glorified Continental omelette. That has now happened, plus a system of team selection that is ridiculous, a view shared by many traditionalists. In spite of unfortunate experimentation, Ryder Cup popularity makes it a top-liner. It is still a prestigious event with a rich tradition. Sam's foresight was right.

The Masters is the showpiece of American golf. It ranks as the first important event of the year, which is not slighting to the preceding tournaments. It merely emphasizes that here is something unique. Everything about the Masters is exclusive. The organization leaves nothing to chance. When the green jacket is donned and the crowds have melted away, post-mortems look for shortcomings. These have to be corrected for the next year. Sometimes new greens are laid.

Above: Max Faulkner and Dai Rees celebrate Great Britain's famous Ryder Cup victory at Lindrick in 1957.

Complaints that sloping greens are too fast can mean reseeding with bent grass replacing the old Bermuda variety. This particular complaint is often true. Fast greens can be like lightning. Once after their last cut, the effect was more like forked lightning. According to readings of the Stipmeter, Augusta greens can show a speed of 12 feet against average tour of between six and seven. In lay language, a suicidal speed. Green alterations can present unknown factors. I remember when drainage problems caused the eleventh to be reconstructed. A dam was made across Rae's Creek behind the lake that rims the green. The drainage problem was solved by laying a network of pipes a foot below the surface through which hot water was pumped. It was felt that this would solve any headache at the 155-yard twelfth. I question whether Tom Weiskopf would agree. It was at this hole that he took a thirteen and a seven in the first two rounds.

There are always surprises, like when Craig Stadler sank a par four for victory, to become part of Augusta's history and an unusual wearer of the green jacket. Stadler was 5 feet 10 inches tall, weighted over 224lb, looked unathletic, had a belly suggestive of bar-darts player, luxuriant moustache that drooped and a reputation for having a fiery temper. Nothing could have been more removed from the image created by men like Jack Nicklaus, Arnold Palmer and Tiger Woods. Nevertheless Stadler proved himself a resolute fighter, an unpredictable professional whose talent had been recognized.

14
Triumvirate 1

The Open Championship was won by *James Braid* for the first time in 1901. In the short space of a decade he claimed the title five times. In 1905 the entry was 152. Bad weather affected play, but Braid's rounds of 81-78-78-81 were good enough to take the Championship in spite of sixes at the fifteenth and sixteenth on the Old Course, St Andrews. On both occasions he drove out of bounds and had to play from difficult lies on the railway track. In 1910, a thunderstorm disrupted play, flooding bunkers and submerging greens, but Braid completed the round in spite of lashing rain and lightning, handing in a card of 77, which he always regarded as the finest round of his career. Unfortunately, the Old Course was pronounced unplayable and the round was discarded. Nevertheless he went on to win with an aggregate of 299.

Braid died in London on 27 November 1950 at the age of eighty. One the few remaining giants of the last century, he formed the Triumvirate with J.H. Tay-

Right: James Braid, Open Champion in 1901, 1905, 1906, 1908 and 1910.

Right: James Braid with Jack White (right) who broke the Triumvirate's domination by winning the Open title in 1904 at Sandwich. He carded the last two rounds in 141 with an aggregate of 296. White's 141 was not beaten until 1935.

Left: J.H. Taylor, dour, dogged, determined.

lor and Harry Vardon and monopolized British golf for twenty years. He was the first to win the Open five times, later equalled by Taylor and beaten by Vardon. A tall, exceptionally powerful player, he was noted for long driving and powers of recovery that became legendary in his lifetime. He held a record of returning a birthday round in a score lower than his age, his eightieth birthday saw him fail by a single stroke. He was one of the founder members of the Professional Golfers Association and was the first professional to be elected honorary member of his Club. To that distinction was added the honour of being made a member of the Royal and Ancient Club, along with J.H. Taylor and Willie Auchterlonie.

A pen portrait of *J.H. Taylor* is not difficult. I think of a sturdy figure, massive boots anchored to the ground, cap jammed down, chin protruding, a dour figure of concentrated energy. There was nothing loose or slip-shod about this five times winner of the Open Championship. Even after he passed four-score years, he still had plenty of physical energy, but was reluctant to leave the quiet and peace of Westward Ho!. Consequently on one occasion everyone had to go to Devon. BBC technicians converted his comfortable sitting-room into a studio, a microphone installed on a desk that he told me was a present from the Artisan Golfers Association for which J.H. had done so much. He watched the presentations with an air of suspicion. We had no script. No rehearsal. We just talked. Reminiscences can become dateless. Different eras were side by side. It was a fascinating experience in a time capsule. On golf in general he regretted the loss of artistry in shot-making instead of relying on graded clubs with mechanical swings. Improvisation was out. In the old days the ball did not flatter you if struck inaccurately. With the guttie a man had to be a real golfer if he wanted low scores. Our talk was a dateless experience. Apart from his record of Championship success, J.H. is remembered as the senior statesman who did more than anyone to improve the status of his colleagues.

Harry Vardon was the dominant member of the Triumvirate. In one season he won seventeen out of twenty-two events and finished second in the others. He is the only man to win the Open Championship six times. Had he not been stricken with tuberculosis the number would probably have been higher. An after-effect of this illness appeared to upset his putting, particularly the short ones. Henry Cotton, ever a shrewd analyst of golfing styles, described Vardon's putting technique as an unbelievable jerking of the clubhead in an effort to make contact with the ball from two feet or less from the hole.

The Vardon grip became popular. The little finger of the right hand overlaps the index finger of the left. To set the record straight, credit for this grip should have gone to J.E. Laidlay, the Scottish international who had used it several years earlier. Vardon had fixed theories about the golf swing. He argued that it was impossible for the left arm to be straight at the point of the swing where so many golfers believed it to be; maybe wishful thinking for his left arm was very bent. High-speed photography shows that the straight left theory is right. Seeing is believing. Some golfers determined that the left arm should be straight find they substitute rigidity instead, with unhappy results. Their action becomes tantamount to playing golf in a straight-jacket. Another Vardon contention was that shot-making was made more difficult if the player refused or was unable to swivel the left hip; as a result the left hip becomes locked and the swing is thrown off balance. On the other hand it sometimes is not as easy as Vardon maintained. He conceded that "golfers find it a very trying matter to turn at the waist, more particularly if they have a lot waist to turn." It is safe to say that players who are bulky in build can still be first-class shot-makers. Lack of suppleness can affect muscular co-ordination which in turn upsets the timing. Modification of the backswing can effect wonders.

Left: Harry Vardon. Unique.

Harry Vardon was a superb striker of a golf ball, the giant of a Golden Age. Between them the first Triumvirate of James Braid, J.H. Taylor and Harry Vardon won sixteen British Open Championships between 1894 and 1914. The second Triumvirate of Palmer, Player and Nicklaus some fifty years later lags behind . . . at least statistically.

15

Triumvirate 2

No individual elevated the status of a golf professional as much as *Arnold Palmer*. He took to the game in the Pittsburgh area, served in the United States Navy, took a degree at Wake Forest, went into business, preferred golf and proved the point by winning the US Amateur Championship in 1954, turned professional and never looked back. In all he collected four Masters, two Open Championships and one US Open title. The influence he has exercised on the game is remarkable. It is only necessary to recall the scenes of "Arnie's Army" sweeping across the fairways to be reminded of the gallery support everywhere he competed. Mark McCormack played a significant part in Palmer's career. McCormack recognized that latent talent and added his marketing expertise and publicity know-how. Together they made a powerful combination. Palmer's golfing

Right: Arnold Palmer.

style was immediately recognizable, particularly the follow-through when the club ended in a whirlwind flourish. The swing was pugnacious and audacious. He had a compulsive loathing of failure. It upset his calculations. With a temperament like Palmer's, there was no joy simply for sentiment. It is difficult to pinpoint the highlights of his career. Safer to take his choices. His best 9-holes were Birkdale 1961 when the sand dunes and fairways faced gale force winds. He carded 31. His nominated best round was Troon, 1961.

Gary Player's record is one long catalogue of success. It includes three Open titles – Muirfield 1959, Carnoustie 1968 and Lytham, 1974; the American Open 1965; two American PGA titles 1962 and 1972; and three wins in the Masters. He was only the third player to win the four major professional events. Competitive golf at this level is an exacting test of physical strength, but the South African, although now in the veteran class, still retains his competitive urge. His style is distinctive with occasional quirks that suggest a mistake, but the result is usually on target. If a golfer swings off his feet at the completion of a drive, anything is possible. In Player's case the ball invariably sails down the fairway. Under pressure he produces pinpoint accuracy. Match-play brings out an aggressive streak that refuses to acknowledge defeat as shown in five wins in the first ten

Right: Gary Player.

years of the World Match-Play Championship and that epic struggle against Tony Lema when he clawed his way back to victory. On a more personal note I remember an evening in his home outside Johannesburg when we went upstairs to his tiny son's bedroom. Sleepily the lad produced a tooth from under the pillow and confided that by morning it would change to money.

If a golfer endowed with powerful back and leg muscles and a pair of sturdy hands is looking for a model on which to base his game, he need seek no further than *Jack Nicklaus*. Here is power golf at its best. Nicklaus for years has personified the maxim that the key to a sound swing is a good grip. The placement of his hands on the shaft is sensitive yet firm. When the hand position of the average golfer is studied, it is clear that lack of control at the top of the swing is invariably due to a weak grip. It is true that Nicklaus has exceptionally strong hands, but hands and arms can be strengthened. Several professionals have developed their muscles by swinging a twenty-two ounce driver. The average driver weighs about fourteen ounces. The difference in weight can give rhythmic hand action.

Jack Nicklaus, the first player to accumulate over £2 million in stake money, is a perpetual phenomenon. If he is not a genius then the word has no meaning.

Left: Jack Nicklaus.

Legends

There is no doubt that *Walter Hagen* inspired and revolutionized the lives of a new generation of professional golfers. He broke down social conventions that down-graded colleagues to second-class citizens. Access into club-houses was denied. Infuriated at being refused entry into the Royal Cinque club-house at Deal during the Open Championship, he retaliated by hiring a Rolls-Royce, parked it opposite the main entrance and entertained friends with champagne and caviar . . .

In many ways Hagen had a dual personality – the professional golfer and a calculating psychologist. His confidence on the links was outrageous. Many times I watched him upset an opponent's concentration by chatting nonchalantly between strokes to spectators without losing his own grip on a match. Projecting his personality had an upsetting effect on some players. You either liked or disliked Hagen. It was impossible to ignore the showman. Physically he commanded attention before a shot was played. Galleries flocked to watch this well-groomed professional with dark hair and sun-tanned chiselled features. His appeal was infectious.

Right: Walter Hagen at the microphone. Henry Cotton is seated on the far right with the Open trophy. On the left Provost Norman Boase and Henry Cullen, R & A Secretary.

Hagen was the first golfer to earn a million dollars and, true to reputation, spent the lot, justifying his extravagances: "I have never wanted to be a millionaire. I just wanted to live like one." To achieve this ambition he won two American Open Championships in 1914 and 1919; four British Open titles in 1922, 1924, 1928 and 1929; but his most remarkable feat was winning four American PGA Match-Play Championships in a row from 1924 to 1927 to make it five in all. He won numberless big money challenge matches, notching up twenty-two consecutive victories over thirty-six holes against America's finest professionals. He had a flair for succeeding when there was most at stake. I remember his flamboyant gesture when at the presentation ceremony following the 1929 British Open victory of handing the winning cheque to his caddie. He played in 1,500 exhibition in eleven years all over the world. His business manager, Fred Corcoran, told me they used to accumulate proceeds in a suitcase before depositing the cash in a bank. On one tour Hagen netted $23,000, but such was his scale of living they ran out of money and had to extend the hotel stay until funds arrived to settle the bill.

Hagen also had a rare ability to forget failure. In 1928 at Moor Park he lost a 72-hole challenge match to Archie Compston by the huge margin of 18 and 17, yet a fortnight later won the third of the British Opens at Royal St George's, Sandwich. He had an ideal temperament and striking powers of recovery. He made difficult shots look easy and, for the benefit of spectators, easy ones seem tough. Long iron shots were brilliant; he revelled in pitching and recovery shots, particularly from bunkers, and had a velvety putting touch.

When his health began to fail, Hagen rarely left his home in Treverse City, Michigan. He died at the age of seventy-seven. To those who knew him, his mem-

Right: Walter Hagen won two US Open Championships (1914 and 1919) and four Open titles (1922, 1924, 1928 and 1929).

Left: The Australian Joe Kirkwood travelled the world with Walter Hagen and was the greatest trick-shot artist of all time.

ory has not faded. He was so dynamic. An appropriate epitaph is a favourite observation that I heard him utter on several occasions: "Never worry... Take time and smell the flowers along the way."

○

Colourful, controversial, colloquial . . . perhaps the most trenchant way of describing this forthright professional. *Archie Compston*, massive in frame, outspoken and direct in speech, was for long one of the attractions of any tournament or championship. His departure to Bermuda was a great loss. Several times he saw the Open title within his reach, particularly at Hoylake, only to see it slip through his fingers.

○

Left: Archie Compston might have been hewn out of granite. He was the favourite professional of the Duke of Windsor.

In golfing circles the name of Auchterlonie has been known and respected for many years. Of the five brothers, all of whom were were keen golfers, two were outstanding. The eldest, *Laurence Auchterlonie*, was born in St Andrews in 1868. He decided to work in America and for several years was professional at the Glenview Club. His eventful year was 1902. He entered for the United States Open Championship at Garden City, Long Island. Increased prize-money attracted an entry of ninety with the bait of £200 for the winner and £970 shared among the first ten places. Auchterlonie liked the new ball which had been developed jointly by Goodrich Company and a Cleveland amateur named Coburn Haskell. The hard rubber core had added some 20 yards to a drive. Auchterlonie's four rounds of 78-78-74-77 not only won the US Open title, but for the first time the winner had broken 80 in all four rounds. In second place came Walter J. Travis, the leading American amateur of that time and designer of the Garden City course. A couple of years later, Travis became the first American to win the British Amateur Championship. Laurence Auchterlonie returned home to St Andrews and finished second in the Scottish Professional Championship of 1919.

Willie Auchterlonie, born in Andrews in 1872, played in the Open for the first time at the age of sixteen, when Jack Burns won the title from an entry of 53 with an aggregate of 171. Five years later, it was his turn to win the Championship with a total of 322. Aucherlonie's equipment consisted of a set of seven clubs he had made himself. Provided a player had mastered the technique of the half-, three-quarter and full shots, they were more than adequate. Not long afterwards, he began the famous St Andrews club-making company. In that 1893 Open his winning aggregate of 322 had been followed by J.E. Laidlay – 324; Sandy Herd –

Right: Willie Auchterlonie (left), 1893 Champion, with brother Laurie, the first man to break 80 in all four rounds of the 1902 US Open. The entry that week was ninety, with prize money of $970.

325; Hugh Kirkaldy – also 326; with Old Tom Morris on 383. Virtually the same entry went to Newcastle, Co. Down, for the Irish Open Champion. Willie Auchterlonie was again the winner with 322; Herd – 325; Hugh and Andrew Kirkaldy tying with 326; J.H. Taylor – 333; Ben Sayers on 335; Harry Vardon – 344; Tom Vardon – 345; and Old Tom on 383. Auchterlonie was appointed Royal and Ancient professional in September 1935, and carried out his duties with courteous efficiency. He laid out the eighteen-hole Jubilee course at Andrews, which was opened in 1946. In 1950 he accepted Honorary Membership of the Royal and Ancient Golf Club, along with James Braid and J.H. Taylor. He died in 1964 aged ninety-one.

○

Right: Ted Ray, a giant in every way. In the historic play-off in the 1913 US Open at Brookline between Ray, Harry Vardon and Francis Ouimet, the twenty-year-old American became the first amateur to win the event.

In 1912 *Ted Ray* won the Open Championship at Muirfield and did so in characteristic fashion. A prodigious smiter, tall and powerfully built, he was not interested in half-measures. He put every ounce of his considerable weight into the stroke, but a distinct forward lunge of the body often caused wayward shots. Cartoonists, particularly Tom Wester, used to show him hacking his way out of a forest of bents and whins. His style was rough-hewn but had definite rhythm in the swing. His recipe is remembered in an oft-quoted answer to one of his pupils who was trying to get more length to his drives: "Hit it a bloody sight harder, mate." Those of us who can look back over many years of championship golf will remember Ray walking across the fairways with hat carelessly placed on the back of his head and puffing clouds of smoke from his favourite pipe. He looked so casual and this happy-go-lucky streak seemed on the surface to run through his game as he wielded his niblick in the rough. The appearance was deceptive. Underneath Ray was a formidable golfer whose skill is preserved for posterity in the records. But it was when he used to describe the early years of his life that his robust humour came to the fore.

He was born in 1877 and used to say that he swung a club as soon as he could walk. His first club was made by his father. The head was one of those wooden pins used by fishermen for mending nets. With the help of a red-hot poker, a hole was made into which was fitted a thorn stick and the club was complete. Ray used to refer to it as the first of the socket type of club. The next stage came when he fashioned his own clubs with a pocket knife from any suitable wood he found in the lanes. His juvenile career ended when he became the owner of the real golf club. He would compare his golf beginnings with those of Sandy Herd, who adapted shinty sticks cut from Strathtyrun Woods, using champagne corks found in a refuse heap behind the Royal and Ancient Golf Club as golf balls, weight being added by inserting screw-nails into the corks. Ray said he would have liked to play Sandy Herd and Laurie Auchterlonie on their childhood links of the cobble stoned streets of St Andrews, with lamp-posts for flags at the cathedral end of North Street. The daydreams of all three boys came true in the Open Championships of America and Britain.

Ted Ray was a giant personality in every sense of the word, almost hewn out of granite. His style was individual to a remarkable degree. He was essentially a natural player, the artistic side of his game being overshadowed by the sheer efficiency of his methods. His long driving and extraordinary powers of recovery became legendary.

○

Left: The diminutive Gene Sarazen, a man with a Cheshire Cat grin, playing against Cyril Tolley at Hoylake.

Diminutive in stature, *Gene Sarazen* has gone through life with a casual air that concealed a shrewd brain. Of pure Italian extraction, he was born in New York State. His first money was earned as a caddie at Apawamis. The records show that he hit the headlines in 1922 for the first time when he won the American Open, having entered from the obscure club of Titusville. Both names were new to the golfing world. Critics dismissed the win as a flash in the pan. Sarazen had other ideas and proceeded to lift the American PGA title by beating Emmett French in the final at Oakmont by 4 and 3.

To tip the scales even further in his favour he beat Walter Hagen in a 72-hole match at Pelham in 1923. Anyone who could do that to Hagen had arrived. And so it was to be. The pocket Hercules of American golf, who was likened to the Cheshire Cat because of his expansive smile, has endeared himself to golfers all over the world by his approach to the fame. In particular, his victories in Britain were extremely popular.

Now in his mid-nineties, this diminutive golfer with an olive complexion still takes impish delight in tossing controversial topics into the arena. Why not greens with holes the size of a bucket? The illegality of certain clubs has always been a popular topic. He has advocated shortening courses so that two hours would be the average time spent on a round. The length ought to be about 3,500 yards with a par of 56, whilst the number of clubs should be limited to five. This would revive the old artistry in shot making. His proposal was not entirely new, but had much in its favour. No doubt he will continue to put forward provocative, stimulating ideas and theories.

○

This photograph of *Allan Macfie* was taken outside the Royal and Ancient and is of historic interest. He won the first Amateur Championship by beating Horace Hutchinson in the 1885 final at Hoylake by the decisive margin of 7 and 6 from an entry of forty-four. Although handicapped by deafness, Macfie showed a lively interest in the game up to the end of his life. He learnt his game at Hoylake and was a perfectionist. "I do not suppose," Harold Hilton once said, "that any player living practised the game so assiduously as Allan Macfie did in those old days at Hoylake. He was full of theories and maintained that to make ball a rise abruptly the eye had to be fixed on the ground immediately in front of the ball. It suited him but imitators ran foul of topping." That may be so, but it does seem to work!

○

George Duncan was a natural genius who would have won more but for his artistic temperament. He revelled in his skill and imagined he could vary his game to play like Hagen, Sarazen, Jones even Compston, but to the onlooker they all seemed the same. An expert hitting the ball with an eloquent swing. Originally he said the swing was flat, but remodelled it on Vardon's method, though it lacked his leisureliness. Duncan was one of the quickest of players, but the action was deceptive. It was instinctive not to hang about. He could play inspired golf, like his final round of 69 at Sandwich in 1922 when 68 was needed to catch Hagen. Sadly 5 went down on the card at the final hole. I like to recall George as the champagne of golf.

○

Bob Andrews was to Perth what Tom Morris meant to St Andrews. His career can be traced to the earliest days of professional tournaments. Born at the North Port, Perth, in 1835, he tried his hand at football and cricket, before turning to golf. His first job was with Mr Condie, a leading figure in the history of Perth golf. Acted as caddie, later promoted to office messenger, which meant afternoon visits to the North Inch with his employer, in his spare time Andrews became expert at approaching and putting. His first success came when winning the first prize at the professional event that marked the close of the St Andrews tournament of 1859. In the inaugural Open Championship he finished 4th. The Perth golfer went to the sleepy fishing village of Hoylake in 1872 for the first important professional tournament held in England. The sixties saw Andrews take part in the longest match of his career. George Gray, secretary of the Royal Club, and Andrews were partners against Major Boothby and a local

Left: Allan Macfie, the first Amateur Champion, outside the Royal and Ancient clubhouse.

ball-maker. The match lasted for six days. Twenty-four holes were played each day, 144 holes in all. At the end of the week the Gray–Andrews partnership had won by eight holes. Many incidents marked his career. In the early match against Tom Morris at Prestwick, he holed out in two with the aid of a fluke. His drive was too strong, scattered the crowds round the green, struck a top hat and rebounded on the green within inches of the hole. On another occasion at a house party given by Mr Condie, wagers were taken that Andrews could drive a ball off the face of a watch. Guests left Blackfriars House for North Inch. Gold watch laid on the first tee, ball placed on the face, Andrews drove within a few feet of the pin.

Right: George Duncan, 1920 Open Champion. After thirty-six holes he trailed Abe Mitchell by 13 strokes. In the end Duncan won the title by 2 shots from Sandy Herd.

The watch was quite unscathed. Bob Andrews began his career with feather balls, clubs elongated and old fashioned, but ignored innovation, preferring his favourite driver, the "Black Doctor". He died in the opening year of the century.

○

Edward Blackwell was born in 1866 in a house on the edge of the Old Course, St Andrews. At the age of five, he was given his first club, a crudely made driver lacking lead and bone. Three years later he played in a competition for the pupils of Dr Browning's School. The winner was Walter Blackwell with 104, Edward came second with 108. At Glenalmond he took advantage of the small course laid out on the cricket fields where play was permitted from summer to Christmas. During school holidays, it was back to St Andrews where his golfing friend was Freddie Tait, who received a half. Blackwell's bag was not overstocked. It consisted of three clubs – driver, iron and cleek, which served as a putter and led to the habit of stabbing the ball instead of following through. Nevertheless, it did not stop him playing off scratch at 18.

In 1885, the Glenalmond chapter closed and Blackwell returned to St Andrews. Shortly afterwards, H.B. Simpson of Brunton arranged a 36-hole marked between Blackwell and Jack Simpson, the Open Champion. Edward won by a single hole. A few days later he left for the United States, where for six years he never visited a golf course. Despite the long lay-off he returned home and won the William IV Medal of the Autumn Meeting with a record card of 82. A further five years in America followed, again without his touching a golf club. Returning to St Andrews, he resumed winning by taking the Calcutta Cup from plus two. That became plus five when he went to Pau in the spring of 1898 and, in partnership with Charles Hutchings, won the Kilmaine Cup for Pau against Biarritz.

Feats such as this were soon forgotten. Instead Edward Blackwell was remembered for the 1904 Amateur Championship at Sandwich, when he lost in the final to W.J. Travis whose putting was inspired. Blackwell disagreed that the title disappeared on the greens. He blamed the forward tees which favoured the shorter-driving American, who otherwise would not have been able to match his opponent's power golf. Horace Hutchinson left a contemporary pen portrait: "Standing above six feet in height, his physique shows the very perfection of strength. Not only is he well endowed but his strength is something out of the common; and it is strength of that special quality that is capable of being exerted in rapid movement. It is doubtless this union of activity and power, combined

Right: Mungo Park, the distinguished nineteenth-century professional who was overshadowed by the more famous Willie Park.

with the ideal orthodoxy of style, that gives him his tremendous length of drive." Judging by old photographs, it is questionable whether purists would agree with Hutchinson's idea of orthodoxy. Blackwell was certainly individualistic in style. The club was held in the palm of both hands, with the left thumb outside, which clearly allowed the hands to slide down the shaft during the swing. At the top of the swing his right elbow was raised to an unusual height. It was a St Andrews swing, though the club was rarely below the horizontal behind the back. Edward Blackwell never had professional coaching; instead he was taught the rudiments by his father, who was a keen golfer. After that he developed his own style, which made him one of the longest drivers. In 1892, he reached the green of the 520-yard fifth hole at St Andrews in two shots, with the wind slightly against, in a match with Major Robert Bethune. Turning around he played the same hole going in and again found the green with his second – more than a thousand yards in four shots with a guttie.

Blackwell also drove from the eighteenth tee on the Old Course to the steps on the left of the green. His longest single drive measured by tape was in 1892 from the seventeenth tee – that was 366 yards with a gutta percha ball. Blackwell's short game improved when he switched to an aluminium putter, though he had difficulty in judging distances. This did not stop him playing for Scotland more than any other man,

Edward Blackwell was a colourful link with the golfing past, though his claim to have known Strath was a trifle forced. It has nothing to do with golf. Apparently Strath fancied Blackwell's nurse and most of their courting took place with the infant Edward in the perambulator, which must have left a somewhat hazy recollection of the legendary St Andrews golfer born in 1836.

○

It is interesting to compare *Douglas Rolland* with Edward Blackwell. The latter was renowned for immense individual drives, but he could not rival Rolland's consistent long hitting. Born in 1860 in Elie, Rolland worked as a stonemason from the age of thirteen and developed pronounced wrist and forearm muscles. Recorded statistics give some indication of his physique. Over 6 feet tall, 41½ inch chest, 12½ inch forearm, 182lb, he was on a par with his even more famous cousin, James Braid, who was born in the same Fife village.

Unlike many of his contemporaries, Douglas Rolland could be casual, almost reckless, in his approach to the game. He enjoyed himself on the links and did not attempt to hide the fact. In an exhibition match against Tom Dunn at

Tooting Bec in London, he arrived in a somewhat mellow mood, in his best clothes, hard-boiled shirt and no golf clubs. Playing with borrowed clubs, he not only trounced Dunn, but smashed the course record in the process, the only cost being a crumpled shirt. In more serious mood, Rolland got backing to accept the challenge issued from Hoylake that John Ball, rated No. 1 in the world, would play any amateur. The Scot finished 9 up at Elie, eventually winning 11 and 10 at Hoylake. A repeat match the next day saw Rolland 5 down with 6 to play, but he managed to win all the remaining holes. Rolland turned professional in 1887. Although highly successful in challenge matches, he never won the Open Championship.

○

Andrew Kirkaldy, better known to an older generation as "Andra", was the natural successor to Old Tom Morris at St Andrews. I recall his native pawkiness, the Fife accent which English ears found somewhat difficult, and his shrewd wit. He was a link between the old and new school of professionals. I remember his criticism after our Walker Cup team had been thrashed: "There's nae muckle wrang with the team. They are a' fit tae win if they are on their game. Gowfers the day are sae muckle in and out ye can never tell when they are going tae be on their game on no. The hale trouble lies in the ba'. The gutta ba wis aye reliable and ye could easy enough pick the best gowfers, but it's no the case today, for I tell ye the ba' beats the gowfers." I can still picture the old professional seated in state by the home green during an Open Championship at St Andrews. If there was any doubt where he was seated, he could be located by the stream of pertinent observations upon golf matters in general. As each couple came up, he would rise from his chair until the business of holing out was finished. He would retire to his chair until the next couple appeared in sight over the Swilcan Bridge. In his closing years I remember him describing what he regarded as the two greatest surprises of his life. First when

Left: Andrew Kirkaldy was born at Denhead, near St Andrews, in 1860. Following the example of his father, who fought in the Crimean War, he joined the Army in 1879, served in the Black Watch, saw action in Egypt in 1882, and again at Tel-El-Kabir. After soldiering, Kirkaldy became professional at Winchester, soon returned to St Andrews. Sound golfer; three times runner-up in the Open, three times third and twice fourth. Sadly he never won the title. He succeeded Old Tom Morris as honorary professional to the Royal and Ancient Club. He will be remembered as a warm-hearted character whose Scottish accent and pawky humour baffled many an Englishman.

70 was broken in a Championship on the Old Course; secondly, when a professional walked across his line of vision resplendent in dinner jacket and studded shirt front. The spectacle was a constant topic of amazement and disdain. He had practical advice for anyone who played golf in snowy conditions. He used to pour liberal quantities of olive oil over the caddie's hair. He could then rub the ball through the greasy locks, thus preventing the snow from clogging!

Andra was a rich personality. There has never been another.

○

Tom Watson's natural boyish grin has appealed to galleries for many years. It never changes. He still retains the image of the college boy who has made good. Without fuss or outward strain he has won the Open Championship five times from only nine entries and stands one victory short of Harry Vardon's total. Sadly the years are catching up. Watson remains a formidable contender. A classical stylist with a power game that produces prodigious distances, the only weakness affects the greenwork. At his peak he had an unerring delicate putting touch, but for the past few seasons putting has become tentative. Short putts can be nightmarish. When the old confidence returns, the magical touch is still there. When that happens, we can be sure that Tom Watson will be eyeing the Vardon target.

○

I would pay tribute to *Jim Barnes* who was born some 120 years ago in Cornwall. It is worth visiting his birthplace. The village of Lelant is not outstanding. There is not much to see. A flurry of little houses and an ancient church, but the effect is pleasing. Tradition would have us believe that it used to be a large town. An historian named Norden tells us in words written over 300 years ago that Lelant was "sometyme a haven towne, but now of late decayed by reason of the sand which has choked the harbour and buried much of the landes and houses; many devises they use to prevent the absorption of the church." The danger persisted and just over a century ago sandstorms almost buried the church. The solution was simple. Marram grass was planted round the church that is set in the heart of the links. Fairways skirt it and greens overlook it. The original 9-hole layout was designed by the vicar of Lelant, the Reverend R. F. Tyacke, who acted as honorary secretary of the club until his death in 1901. It is an enjoyable test of holiday golf on seaside turf. In the clubhouse was, and may still be, a portrait of Jim Barnes.

Younger players will never have heard of the lanky boy who was born in Lelant and used to work in Whiting's shop. His playing record speaks for itself. In the Open Championship he finished sixth when George Duncan won at Deal in 1920; tied with George Duncan for 2nd place at Sandwich in 1922; 9th to Hagen at Hoylake in 1924; won the American Open Championship at the Columbia Country Club in 1921, receiving the trophy from Warren Harding, the American President; in 1925 the Open was staged at Prestwick. Barnes and Macdonald Smith set the pace. The Cornishman began with a 70 for a useful lead. MacSmith

Above and right: The unspoilt, natural Lelant links and the coastline beloved by Jim Barnes. By current standards, the layout may be over-natural but during his years in America "Long Jim" had a hankering for such Cornish scenes. He is remembered still in the quiet clubhouse of the West Cornwall club.

faltered with 76. In the second round Barnes did the same with 77. MacSmith's 69 gave an advantage of two shots. On the last day Barnes was an early starter, but returned a disappointing 79. MacSmith took it easy with 76 and looked set for victory. Archie Compston, Ted Ray and Abe Mitchell were the main threats.

Barnes produced better golf on the final round. He returned a steady 74, but was hardly good enough to win the title. Compston could only manage 75, one shot behind Barnes. Ray tied with Compston with 72. Macdonald Smith needed 78 for victory. It should have been a formality as a partisan Scottish gallery turned out to cheer him home. Crown control as we understand it today did not exist. Spectators had paid their money and were determined to see. Stewards were thrust aside. The Loop became like Piccadilly Circus. The very eagerness of the galleries to see their man win had the reverse effect. Chances were frittered away. In the end a card of 82 meant 4th place. MacSmith had been robbed of the title he wanted most.

Jim Barnes was the only Cornishman to win both British and American Opens. He was also the tallest and probably the thinnest champion in the record books. I mention these facts because a tall, thin man is generally at a disadvantage when it comes to shot-making. Barnes overcame any such physical handicap by taking a widish stance, legs taut, keeping well down throughout the shot. Clubs on the short side, he putted with a cleek, and used a wide stance on the greens. In 1955 Barnes paid a visit to this country from America where he had settled on Long Island. He and I met in Lytham during an Amateur Championship and talked about Lelant. He was looking forward to returning to his birthplace, but feared it might be completely changed. I assured him that Cornwall is one of the few places in Britain that remained unspoilt. In Lelant the sand dunes still creep up to the village. The eighteenth-century sundial with a figure holding an hourglass waits in a niche over the church porch. In the clubhouse his memory and deeds would still be remembered.

○

The death of *Sandy Herd* in 1944 took from the game one of the few remaining giants of the last century. I remember the last time I played with him. It was the championship links of Hoylake. The wind blew strongly from the River Dee. Few men of his age would have persevered. He became tired, the waggles decreased, but finished strongly with one of the draw shots for which he was famous. Several features of his game were distinctive, particularly the waggle. It did not indicate indecision, but marked the psychological moment when the strike was right. He also favoured the old-fashioned palm grip, contrary to the vogue of interlocking and overlapping, but the shot was unquestionably the cut-up with a spoon.

Herd's years of golfing service were spent in England at three clubs, Huddersfield, Coombe Hill and Moor Park, but he was first and foremost a son of St Andrews. He was born in a humble house in North Street on 24 April 1868 and used to say that his first introduction to the game came not on the links but in North Street itself. The course stretched to Bell Street, the holes were lamp-posts which had to be hit by balls made from champagne corks. His companion of similar age was Laurence Auchterlonie. The make-belief dreams they shared at the age of seven years eventually became true. Auchterlonie went to America and won the American Open Championship, while Sandy did the same in England. His professional career was due to David Lamb. At the time Herd was working as a plasterer for Andrew Scott, whose yard produced three Open Champions. Herd received a message from Lamb asking him to go down to the links. A letter from his brother-in-law said that a professional was wanted for the summer months at Portrush. Herd accepted and started work in 1890.

Right: Sandy Herd, Open Champion of 1902, playing with Louis Stanley (left) at Hoylake. He used a palm grip with both hands, wide stance and had limited foot action. Always a formidable match-player, he was the first champion to use the rubber-core ball instead of the guttie. His waggles before driving were legendary. He used to say he knew when the right moment had arrived.

It was the beginning of a highly successful golfing career. He won the Open Championship at Hoylake in 1902 and was runner-up on four occasions. Against that record must be set the fact that from 1900 to 1910 he was playing against the best of three balls, those of Vardon, Taylor and Braid. The Open that he won marked the arrival of the rubber-cored ball. A month earlier the Amateur Championship played over the same links had shown something of the possibilities of the Haskell ball, Charles Hutchings gaining a narrow win over Sidney Fry in atrocious weather. Even so, the professionals refused to accept the new ball and persisted with gutta percha. Herd supported their view, only to change it after a practice round with John Ball. The Hoylake amateur, playing with a Haskell, beat the professional by such a margin that Herd decided to use the new balls in the Championship. He won by a single stroke from Vardon. The margin should have been more, but in the final round Herd became anxious and frittered strokes away.

It was this tendency that cut back Herd's tally to a single Open. Under pressure he faltered. Even so he was second to George Duncan in the 1920 Open Championship. He was then aged fifty-two. Victory was denied by a 7 at the sixteenth. Six years later he won the *News of the World* Tournament, then ranked as the professional match-play Championship, after a tense struggle that ended in his favour at the 38th green, again in a gale force wind similar to the storm that robbed him of an Open win twenty-five years earlier.

1895 was Herd's year. He won practically everything there was to win in the professional world – except the Open. His chances were blown away in hurricane conditions, but subsided to enable Taylor to claim the title. Sandy Herd left behind the memory of a great golfer and warm-hearted character. He was indeed a worthy son of St Andrews.

17

The Tiger Woods Phenomenon

The sensational win by Tiger Woods in the 1997 Masters at Augusta produced an exaggerated reaction from media and commentators. It was prompted by the way the twenty-one year old golfer had outplayed the opposition of the world's greatest players. Mesmerized might be a better description. Woods' display of power-driving was impressive. Long holes became a drive-and-wedge. The spectacle upset everyone. Opposition crumbled. Nick Faldo failed to make the cut. Colin Montgomerie had an excellent start but frittered chances away. After Faldo observed tradition and handed over the green jacket, we were led to believe that a new dimension had changed the game. Future events would be contests for the runners-up slot. Experienced commentators ought to have known better. Obviously Woods in self-confident vein is bound to make a significant impact, but one swallow does not make a summer. Exceptional long-driving is nothing new, but at Augusta it was Woods', pinpoint accuracy that made it so different. It lacked the swashbuckling flourish of Severiano Ballesteros who, in his prime, relied on spectacular recovery shots to repair the damage of spraying shots all over the place. Woods is more clinical. Cool and calculating, he shows remarkable maturity for one so young, though at Augusta there was a hint of vulnerability when he stuttered to 40 for the outward half of the first round, but redeemed the situation on the inward half, finishing one shot short of the record held by Mark Calcaveccia in 1993.

As an individual, Tiger Woods came across as an agreeable personality, intelligent and thoughtful, with a dazzling smile, qualities that attracted the hype that was encouraged by his proud father, Earl, who predicted that his son could collect the Grand Slam of the four major championships. It must be said that in many ways Augusta was ideal for Woods. It suited his style. There were no problems like narrow fairways, intimidating rough or gale force winds sweeping across fairways, as so often happens on British seaside links.

Augusta prides itself in being different, a manicured, weed-free lay out with greens of suicidal pace and cunningly sited holes. It is a law unto itself, controlled by dogmatic officials. Whether Bobby Jones, its creator, would approve the current way of running the event is open to question. He contended that golf is a game to be enjoyed in an ideal setting. Augusta was the answer. Staid, safe and conservative, there was continuity, but 1997 proved different. Placing the green jacket on the back of a coloured man created an unexpected precedent. It had to be accepted. This is not a criticism of the Establishment, just stating a fact.

Woods' technique repays study. It is inevitable to compare his style with John Daly. Here are two men who beat the hell out of the ball by injecting immense power into long shots with different methods. Comparison of physical details shows that Daly is 5 foot 11 inches and weighs 189lb. Woods is 6 foot 2 inches and scales 164lb. It was not possible to see them side by side at Augusta as Daly was a patient in the Betty Ford Clinic, but we know their styles. Daly's power can be attributed to the massive backswing coiling-action. In the case of Woods, acceleration is increased by an immensely fast turn of the shoulders as he hits the ball. A more violent postscript than the familiar Arnold Palmer finish. At Augusta, Woods was averaging 337 yards off the tee. It is spectacular, but it brings with it the danger of burning out physically. Tremendous strain is imposed on the spine that in time takes its toll. The human frame can only take so much punishment. I think of the Irish adolescent wonder, James Bruen, whose backswing defied all tenets. The whirl at the top was somehow ironed out in the downswing with results not unlike Woods', but at the expense of back and wrists. Golfers tried to copy the Bruen method with disastrous results. The same might happen if attempts are made to reproduce the Woods action. Would-be converts will probably be visiting hitherto unknown parts of the course.

At the outset his affairs were supervised by father Earl in spite of not being in robust health after a heart-bypass operation. In due course, Tiger will be exposed to the pitfalls of exploitation. He could also become hostage to human rights agitators, a form of racial discrimination. He is now the champion of an ethnic minority, with Asian blood in his veins from his Thai mother. There is no escape from racial roots. That is not his intention. He has already expressed the hope that further success will benefit black people. He recalled the pioneering efforts of black golfers like Lee Elder and Charles Siffert and acknowledged the debt to their pioneering efforts. He hopes that more young blacks will look on golf as "cool". Unfortunately, the fact must be faced that the game does have a colour prejudice among its older members which would not help such recruitment. There is also the expense of equipment. Sports like athletics, basketball and football have greater appeal, activities in which black players excel and are accepted.

The PGSA membership of some 6,000 has only a few black golfers who appear in tournaments. Sponsorship for ethnic minorities is difficult. The Afro-Caribbean Golf Society, founded a few years ago, has only about seventy members and no clubhouse. It is still an uphill fight to gain recognition. Winning at Augusta did not make Tiger Woods a successor to Martin Luther King.

I hope that Woods' advisors are not activists. The youngster has enormous talent that will mature if left to thoughtful development. There is no need for Leadbetter styling. He is a natural. Glib talk of Grand Slam domination is too early. Maybe it will happen. Recall the tally of past holders of the major titles... Jack Nicklaus has eighteen; Walter Hagen eleven; Gary Player and Ben Hogan nine apiece; Tom Watson eight; Arnold Palmer, Bobby Jones, Gene Sarazen, Sam Snead and Harry Vardon seven each; Lee Trevino and Nick Faldo six. In the light of such accumulative brilliant achievements it is naive to talk about a revolutionary dimension being introduced to the game by this coloured youngster. There is always the danger of achieving too much too soon. Maybe Bobby Jones was sensible to retire at twenty-eight because there were no more pinnacles to scale, but that was in the golden age of legends. On the question of the colour bar in golf, I recall the experience of Joe Louis, when he was world heavyweight boxing champion almost fifty-nine years ago. He entered the San Diego Open Tournament in California, but was informed that the "whites only" rule precluded his appearance. Louis protested. The United States reconsidered the decision and announced that the Louis entry would be allowed as one of the ten conceded to the local sponsors for inviting amateurs. Louis thus became the first black golfer to play in a tournament controlled by the American PGA. Tiger Woods' personality and skills will silence such bigotry. His approach is like a breath of fresh air.

18

Wild Life
on the Links

The mini-boom in golf course construction is satisfying a demand stimulated by the excellent television coverage of championship golf and tournaments, but it is a boom which is liable to be short-lived unless a shortage of courses can be overcome. At the present time there are some 1,729 full-length courses in England, a total that could increase to 1,850 by the end of the century. Official estimates suggest that the overall total for the British Isles ought to be increased by some 700 new lay-outs; in short the target for fresh courses is tough. The English Golf Union has argued that England needs 500 to improve the average of one course for every 40,000. The ratio north of the border in Scotland works out as one per 13,000. Golfers who rely on the facilities of municipal courses now exceed the playing members of clubs and account for 50,000 rounds a year.

Left: Hunstanton links lies by the shore of the River Hun and an intimidating range of sandhills.

Above: Royal Birkdale, with valleys and towering sandhills exposed to the winds. Creeping cloudberry with fruits of a matt blue bloom, clinging willow scrub and yellow evening primrose are encountered in the rough.

Above: Rye in Sussex has an intimidating ridge of sandhills stretching down the length of the links and another range parallel to the sea.

While attempting to ease this shortage of golf courses can only be praised, there are reservations. Inflation, high interest rates, fluctuation in property values have led large scale investors to look elsewhere. A new golf course on its own would be small fry. It becomes a different ball game if the project is an ambitious complex that includes a residential hotel, conference facilities, health club, saunas, tennis and squash courts, riding school, and goodness knows what else, over an area of several hundred acres.

Obviously some of these projects would be first-class, well-organized and popular, but there are enough question marks to stay the hands of planning officers, potential dangers that the Nature Conservancy Council should be quick to spot. The golf course environment contributes richly to landscape and wildlife values. Statistics speak for themselves. The area occupied by golf courses accounts for roughly double that of the Royal Society for the Protection of Birds reserves and over four times the area of the Country Parks. It is important to remember that golf courses provide sanctuary for wildlife at a time when many of our native animal and plant species are under threat from rural and urban environments. It is also good greenkeeping sense to make the best use of the natural processes which formed the courses and help to maintain it. The treadmill of regular fertilising, watering and pesticide dosing can have dire consequences on the natural environment. An example of sensitive management with regard to fertilisers and irrigation is provided by St Andrews Old Course with an average equivalent throughput of 70,000 rounds per year. It has an average expenditure on fertilisers of around £350 and watering only when really necessary. And no one can fault the fine bent/fescue turf.

It is a truism to state that the tradition of golf course management contains a form of land use which is an integral part of the game's natural heritage. The question that has to be asked is whether a course is being managed with wildlife in mind. The answer must come from within the club, particularly the views of the head greenkeeper and knowledgeable members. The weakness is that so few members know or even care what it is all about. It is doubtful whether they know what wildlife features can be found on their course, let alone how they can be safeguarded. A member joins a club to play golf, not indulge in flora and fauna antics. A recovery shot from the rough is not helped if he has to check whether

Above: Gullane, with anti-tank blocks spread across the course. This legacy of World War II was removed by digging trenches into which each one was toppled. The view from Gullane hills offers an inspiring panorama of the Muirfield links, Firth of Forth and Aberlady Bay and the Forth Bridges on a clear day.

the ball is resting next to a rare plant. Admittedly such thoughts could be off-putting, but there is a more serious aspect. This realization is accepted by half of the top courses in Britain which have been designated as Sites of Special Scientific Interest by the Nature Conservancy Council, which advises how their natural heritage can be protected.

To get away from environmental platitudes, let me describe some of the features involved. Royal Troon has, in its semi-rough, plants like burnet rose, lesser meadow rue, sheep's-bit and yellow rattle. In addition, calcareous elements are introduced from shell fragments of marine molluscs that support thyme, kidney vetch, wild carrot and burnet-saxifrage. The fact that semi-rough is mown occasionally helps to maintain its diversity as well as providing a valuable mosaic with scrub of gorse and broom and small patches of heather.

All this may seem over-precious and twee, with little connection to golf, but if we are to be concerned about conservation it has a significance that applies to Royal St George's which is the home of a special species of orchid, the best being the lizard orchid with its strangely shaped grey-green flowers and lizard-like appearance. The seriousness with which environmentalists react could be seen at Gleneagles where Jack Nicklaus designed a new course. It was found that the earthwork operations would have devastated three acres containing raised mires with rare species such as cranberries. After discussions it was agreed that the drainage would be realigned so that these areas could be preserved.

There have been occasions when attempts were made to remedy damage done by man to the scenic environment. Gullane is a classic example of how ugly scars left from the war years can be removed without trace. In 1939 the game at Gullane came virtually to a standstill. Players disappeared. Greenkeeping staff was whittled down to four elderly men. The No. 2 and No. 3 courses were not maintained, except for the greens on No. 2, which were mown whenever possible, but actual playing on both courses ceased. The military took over large areas for defence purposes. Searchlights, gun-posts, pits, miles of barbed wire, all the paraphernalia of coastal defence invaded the fairways. Other areas were marked for training purposes.

During this period of military activity, No. 1 course was almost left alone. Greens escaped damage, but there were some casualties. Concrete anti-tank

Above: Moor Park, laid out on superb park land. The clubhouse was the manor of More, once occupied by Cardinal Wolsey and then Henry VIII, who lodged Catherine of Aragon there at the time of the historic divorce.

obstacles engulfed the 12th hole from tee to green. A metalled road was laid across the course, cutting the fairways of the 7th, 8th, 11th and 14th holes and passing up in front of the 6th green. When the war ended, the road was broken up where it crossed the fairways, the ground soiled and turfed and, in time, there was no sign that it had ever been disturbed. The concrete blocks were a different proposition. In places four feet deep, they stood about 6 feet high with a couple of feet or so below the surface and roughly 5 feet apart. Each block weighed approximately 6 to 7 tons. An estimate showed that over 200 would have to be shifted from the 12th fairway on No. 1 course and 74 from the 12th to No 2 course.

Had they been left as a permanent feature, a novel cross-bunker would have been introduced because players were obliged to drive across a double line of these obstacles at two holes, apart from the hindrance to the centre of the 12th fairway on No. 1. In other parts of the country these obstacles were removed by explosives, a forthright method that removed the immediate difficulty, but cre-

ated further trouble with scattered debris and splinters which caused extensive damage to machines. Gullane had a different solution. The blocks were buried. Holes were dug alongside some of the blocks. The right depth was reached without meeting opposition from rocks. The blocks were levered in. Not a trace remains of this mass burial.

Indirect conservation takes many forms. Sandridge Park is appreciated by golfers without a thought that close at hand are relics of a bygone age when landscaped grounds surrounded great houses. In this case, the relic is an abandoned ice house. In disuse it became a dark, damp cave with instant appeal to pipistrelle bats, timid warm-blooded creatures which

Left: The seaside course of Royal St David's, Harlech, is a natural test of golf. Torrential rain flooded the bunkers during the 1950 international matches.

have suffered from their natural food being poisoned by traces of pesticides and the use of toxic and highly persistent timber treatments in old roofs. Numbers have dwindled to a point where the bats have become endangered, their roosts now being protected by law. Sundridge Park has now a colonized artificial bat cave with a specially designed grille installed at the entrance to the ice house to keep out unwanted visitors.

Finally, I think of the Royal Liverpool Golf Club, its proud traditions linked with famous names, epic championships and a history going back to the days of Young Tom Morris. For those who would see, Hoylake offers the ultimate in appreciation of nature conservancy. My mentor was Guy Farrar, for many years Secretary of the Club and an authoritative ornithologist. From him I learnt the secrets of that vast stretch of wet, glistening sand, an estuary five miles wide from Red Rocks to the Point of Ayr on the Welsh side, with a backcloth of the hills and peaks of North Wales. It is a sanctuary for wildlife, a place of many moods. The summer tide creeps over the sun-baked sands with scarcely a ripple and the

Welsh mountains are hidden beneath the veil of a heat haze. In the autumn it becomes a carpet of hostile grey water whipped by the west wind with foam and spray. In winter, mud banks are frozen between the tides, with gutters half-choked with broken ice and march grass coated white. Throughout there is teeming bird life.

Dunlin, knot and ringed plovers feed heads down along the water's edge. They race hither and thither on twinkling feet dibbling briskly. Suddenly they rise as one, swing out over the water, twist and turn, straighten and with a tremendous rush of wings, swing right-handed and sharp with a flash of white and land on the spot they had left. A forest of flickering wings, and again they are busy feeding. Three grey plovers stand rather limply and pick at the mud spiritlessly. Close to them a flock of redshank, feeding busily, all moving one way. A little further out, a small party of golden plover and their attendant dunlin. And beyond them a long line of oyster-catchers. They move in with the tide, feeding until there is no mud and they are belly deep in water. Then they rise suddenly as one, wheel out over the water, bank, a flash of white, and away to find more food. It is this feature that is compelling, a sight that only a few of the golfers, who quietly continue their round on the other side of the dunes, occasionally appreciate. Hoylake always reminds me of these aerial manoeuvres of large flocks in which every bird banks, swerves, dives and turns at right angles as one. With each turn they change colour, so that a flock at a distance shimmers, is now visible, now invisible, now all white breasts, now all dark back, now just nothing. Suddenly the flock skims the waves, rises abruptly, a cloud against the sun and rains down to the saltings. Each bird instantly becomes an entity, dibbling hither and thither, twittering contentedly.

This wild, plaintive, yet measured and liquid cry is a reminder of how much we owe to the combined forces of imaginative golf clubs and co-operative environmentalists. One thing puzzles me about this Hoylake scene. The cattle in Charles Kingsley's poem, which Mary was bidden to call home across the Sands o' Dee, must have been grazing on these saltings, but I cannot believe that Mary, a local girl, could have allowed herself to be surrounded by the tide and drowned. It is a sad thought, but the lass must have been very stupid!

Right: Turnbury – wonderful linksland overlooking the tail-end of the Firth of Clyde and the granite dome of the island Aisla Craig, breeding ground of the gannet. Further off is Arran, the Mull of Kintyre and, on a clear day, the distant coast of Antrim, near Portrush.

19

Visual
Instruction

The name of Mabel Stringer means little to golfers today, yet she was an influential pioneer in the development of women's golf. Describing herself as "the first woman to write on golf as a profession", she did so with a clarity and accuracy. Many of her descriptions are difficult to imagine. How a first-class caddie had 9*d.* a round, with 6*d.* for lunch and 3*d.* for tea; a second-class boy earned 6*d.* per round; if the same lad was employed for the week, including Sundays, with as many rounds as one pleased, the cost was 15*s.* 6*d.* Tips were moderate. Boys were always satisfied with what they were given. She later deplored that caddies could command 5*s.* per round, be aggrieved at a 2*s.* 6*d.* tips, and expect lunch money. An open meeting could cost a player as much as a pound note. Halcyon days for some, but others were not so fortunate. When Mabel Stringer began her journalistic career, the activities of women in golf events were treated as items of social interest rather than suitable for the sporting columns. On a time-scale she bridged the centuries, being present at the second British Championship of Littlestone in 1894 and the Curtis Cup match at Prince's, Sandwich, in 1956. Mabel retired in 1924. Friends presented a cheque from a collection amounting to £166 6*s.* 6*d.*, which she used to install electricity in her Kent cottage, where she died in 1959 aged eighty-nine.

This hark back to the past was prompted by an announcement of the current grand total of stake money to be won. The figures are unbelievable, mirroring the trend that has taken place in such a comparatively short span of time. I

Near right: Max Faulkner, Open champion, Portrush, 1951.

Far right: Jack Burke Jnr., American Ryder Cup player, winner of Augusta Masters, 1956.

Unless the first quarter of the backswing is correct, the chances of the shot being successful are slight. In both these style studies the action is copybook. The left shoulder is beginning to move round, underneath the chin. Left leg commencing the pivot. Weight shifting from left to right foot. Clubhead swung back by arms and not lifted by wrists. No suggestion of snatching the club up with wrists.

also came across a feature focusing on Max Faulkner, the extrovert winner of the British Open in 1951. Now in his eighties, Max is still interested in sea-fishing, a different setting to those heady days when he contributed to the epic Ryder Cup win at Lindrick in 1957. He seems very happy and does not complain that the financial rewards for his Open success were chicken-feed alongside the sums realized by Nick Faldo, Colin Montgomerie and Tiger Woods. Envy was never a Faulkner failing. He was a genuine carefree character who brought real enjoyment to the professional scene.

Those of us who were part of the scene are conscious of the discrepancy between then and now. It is difficult to realize that the sophisticated set-up of today's championships and tournaments is comparatively recent. I recall when caddies did not wear identifying numbered arm bands or jackets with identifying names; how spectators often did not know who they were following, the score, or state of the match. It was all so casual. At St Andrews, where the organization was expected to be beyond rebuke, the draw for the next day's play in the Open was posted in a back window of the Royal and Ancient clubhouse. If there was a delay, people just waited. The information was vital, not only for the implications of the draw, but the system of putting all the names into the bag meant that a current leader might come out first, last or the middle. Communication with outlying parts of the course was primitive. Caddies were hired to act as messengers. Telephone facilities were usually

Right: Sam Snead, swing frozen at top of backswing. Left shoulder underneath chin. Full shoulder pivot. Left arm straight. Firm left hand grip. Wrists cocked. Right elbow nicely down. Right leg braced. His partner, Ben Hogan, an interested observer.

a public call box at the rear of the Press tent. Hole-by-hole accounts were pieced together from the chair of runners. Those less fortunate foot-slogged from match to match and hoped for the best.

Changes came about in 1963. The tented village appeared for the first time at Dalmahoy for the Senior Service tournament. The innovation meant restaurants, bars, closed-circuit television, hot and cold running water, flush lavatories, plus tubular-steel stands, and a complete information service from the course. It marked the end of the beer-and-curled sandwich tent, and hessian screened lavatory facilities. The improvements were long overdue. Spectators were regarded as something of a nuisance with no rights. We now have creature comforts, occasionally four-star standard, but the cost has meant extortionate entrance fees. The spectator is almost fleeced, and has become the Cinderella of the fairways. He must watch at a distance, regimented, regulated and relegated to areas where his presence is not a distraction. At a price, there are so-called grandstand seats from which play can be watched, possibly even rewarded by a professional gratuitously tossing a ball in their direction. The scenario has become standard. Bossy stewards, endless white lines, one-way traffic, and army of so-called officials sporting badges and arm-bands, uniformed commissioners supervising behaviour and protocol. Cameras are forbidden. Everything is pompous and negative. Every year patient spectators have to pay more to watch over-touchy, over-protected and over-rewarded professionals.

Would-be spectators would do well to ask whether they are getting value for money. A hefty chunk is needed to watch the British Open Championship. Following a top match is a strenuous business if every shot is to be watched. Anyone who tries will find it a fool's game. A charging army of spectators hoping to get a vantage point finds such gazebos already occupied by patient galleries. The answer is strategic spectating on television. It is cheaper, more comfortable and a revealing solution, although sadly lacking the electric atmosphere of actually being there. Nevertheless, you can see the strain and reactions of the participants, even the whites of their eyes at moments of tension, disappointment and delight, all good dramatic stuff.

The improvement in television coverage over recent years has been remarkable. Camera-work is excellent, although some commentators tend to forget it is not a chat show. Nothing is more off-putting than a smoothie referring to players in terms that suggest a close, if not intimate, friendship. Colloquial slang is all right in its place, but is a cheap substitute for restrained and knowledgeable descriptions. Self-induced familiarity does not impress. It detracts and distracts. I remember once at Walton Heath during the European Championships when an interviewer broke the concentration of players during important rounds to ask their views on the course. As the professionals in question were possible winners, the intrusion was fatuous. Another television series that came under a similar heading was the Pro-Celebrity programme. It seemed a novel idea, but the spectacle of the same two Americans saddled with duff partners soon became an aimless exercise.

Below: Billy Casper.

Centre: Louise Suggs.

Right: Jack Nicklaus.

To return to the subject of strategic spectating on television, it is possible to convert the exercise into sessions of self-tuition, provided that you know what to look for. The basic points are there to copy. The discerning viewer can benefit from what are virtually visual coaching lessons from the game's top players. Assimilate certain principles and shot-making will improve.

No round should begin without a warm-up spell. Stiff muscles strangle any swing. Jack Nicklaus stretched his muscles with the aid of an iron, at the same time letting his body turn to and fro as if playing a shot. Billy Casper, 1959 US Open champion, has a similar exercise. Louise Suggs, 1947 US champion and 1948 British title holder, has a routine check of shoe spikes.

Preliminaries before shot-making repay close study and analysis. Individualistic mannerisms mean something to the player concerned, but there is one thing they have in common. Every time a shot is lined up, the same preliminary drill is followed, a standard routine well worth studying. The player puts the right foot forward, checks the line of flight, then soles the club behind the ball. The left foot is in the stance position and the grip looks as firm as if it is moulded to the shaft. Individual mannerisms are plentiful but the basic principles are standard practice.

The grip is all important. If the hands are wrong, the entire swing is affected. A golfer is only as good as his hands. A shot is determined by the way

Near right: Billy Casper.

Far right: Bob Charles, first winner of Open Championship by left-handed player, 1963.

Adopting a set drill of pre-stance actions is valuable. It creates a sense of rhythmic purpose. It helps to co-ordinate mind and muscle, mentally shaping and playing the shot before actually squaring up to the ball.

Near right: Peter Oosterhuis.

Far right: Peter Oosterhuis, four times winner of the Harry Vardon Trophy.

the hands are placed on the shaft. Hands vary so much in size and shape that grips often look different when they are orthodox. There are the recognizable grips: overlapping, interlocking and palm, with several variations, but irrespective of the grip chosen, one feature is constant. Notice the left hand on the shaft. The right hand can vary, but the left is firm, not over-tense or slack. It is a genuine grip with no danger of the shaft turning in the hands when the clubface makes contact with the ball. The swing is dependent upon the way you hold the club.

If a faulty grip can ruin a swing, a faulty stance is equally disastrous. The stance is the foundation of the swing. The first thing to notice on the television screen is that no player straddles the ball with feet too wide apart, a failing so

Near right: Peter Thomson, the Australian who won the Open title three years in succession, at Hoylake in 1956.

Far right: Arnold Palmer.

Near right: Frank Stranahan.

Far right: Arnold Palmer.

Individualistic drill before a stroke is played. Soling the club behind the ball is often the first step. Remember, if the club rests on its heel or toe, the club could twist in the hands as heel or toe make contact with the ground. It is like driving a car on two wheels. Many players, like Frank Stranahan and Arnold Palmer, put the right foot forward, look at the line of flight, place the left foot in its stance position, and check the grip until it feels that both hands are moulded to the shaft. These points may seem trifling, but remember that the greatest golfers do not waste time and thought on inessentials.

common among golfers. It gives a feeling of security, but makes full pivot impossible. The shot becomes a shoulder-and-arm-affair with the back muscles locked, curtailing the left side and hip swivel. A foolproof tip can be checked on the screen. The feet should be about the width of the shoulders for a full shot with the weight evenly divided. The distance narrows as the shot gets shorter, but do not creep ahead of the ball.

Another pointer: note the comfortable way in which the player's arms hang from the shoulders. There is no hint of reaching for the ball. Neither is the ball addressed too far forward when the left foot carries too much weight. The rhythm of the swing becomes upset through the difficulty of transferring weight to the

Near right: Henry Cotton.

Far right: Ronnie White.

Stance and grip are important, especially the position of the body in relation to the ball. Relaxed knees of all four men ease any suggestion of body tension. Toes point out slightly. Arms hang naturally from the shoulders with the club acting as a natural extension, a position that generally makes a grooved swing easier. The wrists have full flexibility to act as a hinge linking arms and hands with the shaft and clubhead.

Near right: Gary Player.

Far right: Bob Charles.

right. The shot will be topped. In wood shots note how the ball is addressed at a point opposite the left heel. For irons the ball is played a few inches back from the left heel.

Another tip to study and copy is the straight line at the address that can be drawn from the left shoulder to the ball. The club virtually becomes an extension of the arm. Tee-height is often far too low. It can be a contributory factor to indifferent tee-shots. One way to restore confidence is the leave the driver in the bag and use a 2-wood. Notice how the upper half of the ball appears above the clubhead. The result can be a marked improvement in wood play. Peg-tees with irons means a loss of backspin. Even so, incisive shot-making is adequate compensa-

Near right: Chi-Chi Rodriguez, volatile Puerto Rican professional.

Far right: Reginald Whitcombe, rugged winner of the 1938 Open.

Near right: Fred Haas.

Far right: Johnny Palmer.

Check tee-height. Usually far too low. If you lack confidence in the driver, leave it in the bag, take a No. 2 wood and use a tee that shows more than half of the ball over the top of the clubhead.
In the studies of Haas and Palmer, a straight line could be drawn from left shoulder to the ball. The Americans' clubs have become an extension of the arm. It is a maxim that position at address and impact is virtually identical.

tion, but note how the stance is closed and the swing more upright.

Bobby Jones once said that the correct use of the hands and wrists is one of the easiest things in the world to visualize, but is about the most difficult to describe in print. The television screen bridges that gap. Watch the wrists for the first movement of the backswing. There is no suggestion of snatching up the club with the wrists like the average golfer's chopped action. Instead, the club is pushed back with the left hand, wrist, arms and side. The left arm stretches and extends, not with poker-like rigidity, but an easy, natural reaching out. The right foot is firmly based, taking more weight as the left hip turns. The wrists begin to cock and the right elbow comes into the side. It is all there to see. If the back-

The second stage; turning left hip to the right, start of weight transference to the right foot. No attempt to snatch the club up. Head still. Left shoulder beginning to shift around under the chin. Wrist-cock beginning.

swing is right, the odds are that the downswing will be right, but the first quarter of the backswing determines the fate of the shot.

The top of the backswing produces some significant pointers. The hips come round and the body is wound up in preparation for the downswing. This comes across clearly on the screen, with the emphasis on the pivot. Many golfers regard this movement as an artificial turn of the body, instead of seeing it as the natural way to position the body before injecting power into the shot. Some of the criticism is sour grapes. Watching supple professionals can be discouraging if a thickening waist has made it impossible to achieve a 90° turn from the address. Even so, the pivot, modified and curtailed if necessary, is absolutely essential.

Check the shoulder pivot. Ball is sighted over the left shoulder. Shoulders at right angles to the line of flight of the ball. Shoulder-pivot plus the hip winding up are essential in a sound swing.

Top row (left to right): George Archer, Norman von Nida, Jack Nicklaus.

Bottom row (left to right): Dick Mayer, Gene Littler, Bob Charles.

Another point to notice is the firmness of the grip. Cocked wrists and a firm grip are essential at the top of the backswing. It looks easy to copy, but there are pitfalls. Many golfers let the club drop below the horizontal. When that happens the chances are that the wrist-cocking is out of control. The grip is too relaxed. The shaft is held by the finger tips. The player is deceived by a feeling of freedom of movement. The hint of a newly found suppleness is a snare and delusion. What happens is that in the downswing the grip has altered. At impact the grip turns in the hands. It is easily checked. Sole the driver in the address position immediately after playing a shot. If your fingers have to let go, the grip must be corrected. Remember that you are only as good as your hands. Firmness of control must be

Check-points at top of backswing. Wrists must cocked, grip firm, otherwise at impact the club, having turned in the hand, will be different from what it was at the address.

retained at the top of the backswing without loosening the fingers. On the screen, look for the left hand and the last three fingers. The shot depends on the firmness of the grip.

The shoulder-pivot separates the tigers from the rabbits. Television is an excellent medium for featuring this segment of the swing with the greatest players as demonstrators. At that point note how the ball is sighted over the left shoulder. The shoulders are at right angles to the line of flight of the ball. The entire movement looks effortless, which is in contrast to the long-handicap golfer who relies on his arms, snatched swing and a half-hit shot. The cure is eminently practical. Study the action shots on the screen for confirmation, and then vet your

Top row (left to right): Fred Daly, Billy Joe Patten, Lee Trevino.

Bottom row (left to right): Yoshiro Hayashi, Ed Oliver, Eric Brown.

The clubhead is behind the hands in the downswing. The uncoiling of hands, arms and body, uncocking of wrists, and transfer of weight to the left foot are all part of a rhythmic movement that gathers momentum.

own method by holding the action at the top of the backswing and by checking your shoulder-turn.

Contradictory theories have been put forward about the value of a straight left arm at the top of the backswing. Harry Vardon had no doubts. He said, "I am firmly convinced that there is no such thing as a straight left arm at the position where so many golfers have been informed there is."

Had he watched an Open Championship on television, his argument would have been modified. It is worth recalling that Vardon's left arm was very bent. There is sample evidence that a straight left arm is an important part of the top players' swing. On the other hand, it is true that some well-known golfers favour

Top row (left to right): Charles Ward, Alfred Perry, Ben Hogan.

Bottom row (left to right): Lloyd Mangrum, Jim Turnesa, Byron Nelson.

Body power co-ordinates with the hands. Tucking in of the right elbow ensures that the full force of the shot is generated and transmitted through the hands. Acceleration of clubhead speed is terrific.

a slight bend in the left arm at this point of the swing. Both techniques produce copybook shot-making.

While there is flexibility about the straight left arm theory, there is general agreement about the role of the left arm in the downswing. It is most important in the first stage of the downswing. If this is not accepted, the right arm takes command too soon. The left arm position can be checked on the screen, the pulling-down action by the left shoulder, with the arm and hand clear. There is no hint of hitting from the top of the backswing. Note how the left arm and side are firm at impact. They take the full force of the thrust by the right leg, back and arm without crumbling. The left hand supplies the control. The right hand infuses

The bent right side indicates the power generated. Head still anchored. The lateral shift takes the hips round in smooth fashion. The natural flowing action of the shot brings the body face onto the line of flight

the power. Both of the hands co-ordinate in order to work as one.

Immediately after impact there are several points to note and copy. The left side moves part of the way, allowing the hands to flow through without interruption. The head is anchored. The hips are coming round to face the hole. The club hits through the ball. There is no restriction of leg action. Note how the head is anchored, although the ball is well on the way. There is no suggestion of looking up too soon. The players hit past the chin, which points to the spot where the ball was.

Several lessons can be learnt from studying players at the completion of a shot. Television is particularly useful because it focuses attention on the player to the exclusion of outside distractions. The upright position is noticeable. This

No restriction to the follow-through. Flowing action of arms and club brings the body round in fluent fashion. Grips still firm, particularly the left hand. These finishes indicate balance and poise. Follow-through is essential.

erectness indicates that the legs were "under" the player at all stages of the swing. The full sweep of both arms shows the natural finish. The position of the feet is also instructive. The weight has been allowed to come through fully and easily on the left foot. There is no sign of the common complaint of pulling the left foot away and falling back. In many ways the follow-through is the backswing in reverse.

Generally speaking, the players who are featured on television personify three important factors that count in golf: concentration, confidence and relaxation, and, of course, they all have their own fingerprints of style. Watch with intelligent eyes. The benefits can be considerable. Seeing is much better than

Right: John Jacobs, Ryder Cup captain, golf instructor to champions.

Gene Sarazen once said, "All the books in the world, and instructions from the greatest professionals in the game won't teach the average man and woman how to play a first-class game of golf unless they are willing to give up a certain amount of time to practice." True words.

Near right: Arthur Lees.

Far right: Sam Snead.

reading, but it is useless unless you know what to look for. If you search for too much detail, confusion will inevitably result. The best way is to decide beforehand which points you are going to study. Keep to those. Do not be tempted to look at everything. With practice you will be able to distinguish between effect and cause. By degrees you will see the effortless simplicity of the game. At its best the golf swing is a natural action. Trimmings are individualistic, but you must watch intelligently.

Practice must be intelligent. Now what you our doing? If a mistake is made, check what has happened and how it can be corrected, otherwise you are only practising your faults.

Left: Gary Player giving professional advice on the practice-ground.

Left: Robert Halsall, for many years professional at the Royal Birkdale Golf Club, alternating in the winter months with similar duties at the Monte Carlo Golf Club at Monaco, an appointment originally arranged with Henry Cotton, watching Norman von Nida having early morning practice before a championship begins.

20

The Ultimate Stroke

here is much to be learnt from watching techniques on the green, but it must be an intelligent assessment. If you do not know what to look for, you are only wasting your time. It is pointless to miss out on a unique opportunity, for everything you need to know is there to study. Nothing is hidden. The choice is endless. The methods used are as individualistic as the players holding the putter. There is no set method. Grips can be cross-handed, reverse overlap, one handed, both hands well down the shaft, and so on. Putters can range from 12 inches to a shaft so long as it rests against the chest. The permutations are there, but certain basic features have to be observed.

You never see a tense grip. That automatically kills a sensitive touch. Once the "feel" of a putt is gone, you might just as well switch to hockey. On the other hand, a "feather" grip can be equally disastrous. It lets the shaft turn in the hands at impact. To be dogmatic about the stance is dicey. There are so many variations, each liable to be changed at short notice. Soling the putter in front of the ball at address in favoured by many top players. The ritual inspires confidence as well as acting as a muscle rehearsal for the putt. Playing technique favours orthodox movements – blade square to the line of the putt and taken back low with a slow rhythm. Stabbing is out. Head anchored, shoulder and hip movement elim-

Right: Ronnie White. Fingerprints of style in putting are as individual as the person holding the putter. There is no set method. One feature is constant. You never see a tense grip. This was the one that worked wonders for Ronnie White, the outstanding English amateur.

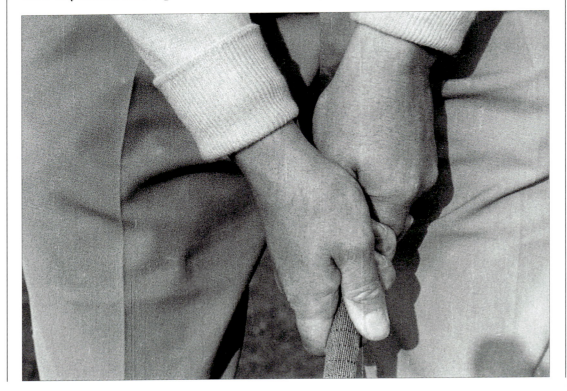

inated. No hint of the long handicap golfer's failing of "head-up" and a half-topped putt with the left hand turning over at impact. Curing that fault would in itself justify learning by watching. The follow-through is a flowing movement with the blade hugging the ground and following the line of the putt, not a meaningless postscript, but an unhurried completion of the stroke.

Reading the greens repays attention. The routine varies: some players are quick and decisive, others flop about for what seems like hours, but the drill is useful. Contours and slopes are studied, particularly within a few feet radius of the hole. The line examined from behind the ball and the grain of grass checked. The drill is important. Reading the green is the only way to putt intelligently, but

This page: Interesting sequence showing the grip used to great effect by Stanley Bishop when US Amateur champion. Note how the putter lies across the fingers of the right hand. The left thumb nestles comfortably between shaft and right hand.

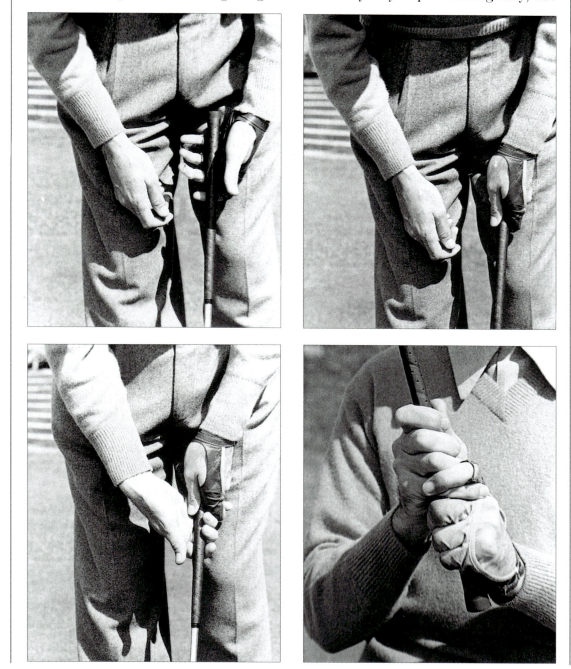

you must know what you are doing. Set the routine. Keep to it every time you putt. Remember the ball runs further with the grain; conversely the pace is slower against. If the grain is left to right across the hole, the putt is played slightly to the left. Grain right-to-left means striking the putt a little to the right. An easy check is to detect shine on the green. If it can be seen from behind the ball, then the putt will be with the grain. Gauging the pace of the green is all-important and can only come with practice. Decide the line and strike the ball so that it rolls over a point selected about a yard from the ball. Missed putts are usually caused by misreading, not mishitting. In windy conditions, the borrow is anticipated by playing from the windward side of the tin. There is no need to be self-conscious.

Right: Ben Hogan studies a difficult last putt green.

The routine procedure of "reading the green" is vital. The best method is to follow a fixed order until the drill becomes almost automatic. If the line is difficult to pick out, it is often best to sight the back of the hole.

Right: Ronnie White shows how to get down to a task.

Get down behind the ball and study the line. Practice is the only answer. It breeds confidence. Putting is 75 per cent confidence.

Now for an insidious complaint that undermines the confidence of even the greatest golfers when faced with a straightforward putt. This psychological block, known as the "yips", has wrecked many a career. Symptoms vary, but usually the right hand takes control on short putts and jerks the putter-head through. The ball is nudged off line and invariably over-shoots the mark. On fast greens the trouble becomes more aggravated. In America this phenomenon is known as the "twitch". Once a player is stricken, the odds are that it becomes a fact of life. Simple putts are dreaded. Anything can happen and usually does. The cure is so elu-

Left and below: Henry Cotton was meticulous in checking the line.

"yips". The putter nose is in the air and the ball is struck with the heel of the centre-shafter club, tantamount to driving a car on two wheels. Critics are silenced by the results, but it is dangerous to copy.

I remember how Leo Diegel used to putt with outstretched elbows, the right elbow acting as a hinge, with the ball forward, straight, still wrists and the club pressed against his chest. Gene Sarazen played the putt off the right foot with the right index finger down the shaft. For a time Henry Cotton adopted a double-handed putting grip. Alfred Padgham, who one season (1936) not only won the British Open Championship but every major tournament, owed the success to skill on the greens. He maintained that the putt was the same as the drive with

Right: Tony Jacklin, Open champion 1969, US Open winner 1970.

Left: Arnold Palmer uses short backswing.

Left: George Archer, somewhat ungainly putting style for such a big man.

easy stance, slow backswing and fluent follow-through. He had no nerves, which phlegmatically made him immune to the "yips".

The search for the ideal putting style never ends, which perhaps is just as well. Bobby Jones, who analysed shot-production with clinical thoroughness, came out in favour of the pendulum theory. To quote his words: "unquestionably a pendulum-like swing, precisely along the line of the putt and suspended from a point exactly over the ball, furnished the ideal conception of accurate striking. But so long as human toes stick out in front and until a golf club turns into a croquet mallet and can be swung backward between the legs, there is little hope of this being attained."

Right: Roberto DeVicenzo of the Argentine, Open champion 1967.

Right: Cary Middlecoff, 1956 US Open champion.

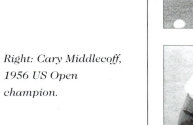

Left: Gene Littler, US Open and Amateur champion.

Lord Brabazon, as was his wont, took the matter further. He constructed an automatic putter. It took the form of a heavy tripod. The swinging pendulum was so designed that every putt was struck with exactly the same force and direction. From 6 feet he found that every putt went straight into the hole once the line had been established. Increasing the range to 12 feet did not affect its reliability. This seems to confirm the pendulum theory claim.

Experiments with putter design are endless. The iron putter served as an alternative choice to the wooden putter which it resembles in stiffness and uprightness. The Schenectady putter was used by Walter Travis when he won the British Amateur Championship at Sandwich, only to be made illegal in its coun-

Right: Jimmy Adams.

Left: Richard Chapman and Jimmy Adams used distinctive stances. Chapman played off the right foot.

Left: A crucial putt by Henry Cotton at Muirfield, when he won his last Open.

try of origin. If reputations are any guide, one of the greatest putters of all time was Willie Park, Jnr. Dispensing words of wisdom about the art of putting, he never underestimated his domination: "I give all the knowledge that won for me the position of the best and most consistent putter in the world – I was highly successful and the great strength of my game was my ability to hole, with certainty, putts from two to three yards." If only Lyle, and for that matter, Woosnam, had such a belief in his ability. Park spoke as a member of the famous Musselburgh golfing family. His father won the Championship Belt in the inaugural event of 1860 and again in 1863 and 1866. After Young Tom Morris won the Belt three times in succession (from 1868 to 1870), the familiar open trophy was won by Willie's uncle, Mungo Park, in 1874. It was Park Senior's turn in 1875, with young Willie taking the title in 1887 and 1889. When J.H. Taylor of Winchester became the first English professional to win the Open five years later, Willie challenged Taylor to a man-to-man match and beat him, to the satisfaction of Scotsmen who resented English intrusion.

Willie Park's putter, shallow-faced, wry-necked and slightly lofted, had a long shaft so designed to cope with cuppy lies. Favouring a stance in front of the ball, his advice was lucid: "I keep the club just clear of the ground. I hit only the ball, never the ball and the ground, and by keeping the club clear of the ground, I hit the ball high on its centre, thus making it keep close to the ground on the way to the hole." His stance was distinctive. He stood with the left foot completely withdrawn, the ball only five inches from and just in front of the right toe. The club was held at the bottom of the grip. He crouched over the ball and used only his wrists. He said he never saw the hole when he hit the ball and never looked up until it had time to drop in the hole. One thing is certain. The method worked on greens that were nothing like the current velvety surfaces. Had he had such luxury, Willie might have been even more successful.

The quickest way to improve putting is to master the art of reading the greens. It is not a "show-off" gesture. The greatest golfers of many decades have followed the drill. With intelligent concentration, it can improve putting.

Right: Arnold Palmer despairs of Ken Venturi's greenwork.

Left: Jack Nicklaus listens to Tony Jacklin's woes.

Postscript: Sometimes it is timely to remember that golf is essentially a simple game made complicated by theorists!

Index
of Names